Consumer Nationalism in China

Consumer Nationalism in China

Examining Its Critical Impact on Multinational Businesses

Maggie Ying Jiang

ANTHEM PRESS

Anthem Press
An imprint of Wimbledon Publishing Company
www.anthempress.com

This edition first published in UK and USA 2024
by ANTHEM PRESS
75–76 Blackfriars Road, London SE1 8HA, UK
or PO Box 9779, London SW19 7ZG, UK
and
244 Madison Ave #116, New York, NY 10016, USA

British Library Cataloguing-in-Publication Data
A catalogue record for this book is available from the British Library.

Library of Congress Cataloging-in-Publication Data: 2023950925
A catalog record for this book has been requested.

ISBN-13: 978-1-83998-285-9 (Hbk)
ISBN-10: 1-83998-285-3 (Hbk)

Cover Credit: Maggie Ying Jiang

This title is also available as an e-book.

CONTENTS

TABLES

ACKNOWLEDGMENTS

I wish to express my deepest gratitude for the completion of this book, a project that consumed the past three years of my life. Balancing this endeavor with a substantial amount of professional responsibilities and the duties of motherhood for two children made this journey an intricate juggling act. Throughout this time, the unwavering support of my family was crucial in navigating these challenges. Their understanding, encouragement, and sacrifices provided the foundation upon which this work has accomplished.

This book stands as a testament to their unwavering support and belief in my aspirations. Their presence and understanding during moments of limited time and overwhelming commitments were the pillars that sustained my dedication.

I am also grateful for the invaluable guidance and support received from various sources throughout this journey. Your contributions and insights have enriched the content of this book and shaped its final form.

To everyone who played a part, knowingly or unknowingly, in this journey, I extend my heartfelt appreciation. Your collective support has made this achievement possible, and I am deeply thankful for each contribution.

Chapter 1

INTRODUCTION

The current geopolitical context presents significant challenges for multinational companies (MNCs), especially those operating in countries that have disputes with their home country. This complexity is further intensified for MNCs in China or those heavily reliant on the Chinese market. The recent joint statement by G7 leaders emphasized the need to "de-risk" from China, acknowledging that completely "decoupling" any major economy from China is nearly impossible (Lee, 2023). As a result, there is now a widely recognized consensus on the importance of "de-risking" strategies when engaging with China across a wide range of countries (Gewirtz, 2023).

However, the interpretation and application of the term "de-risk" vary among different nations due to the inherent ambiguity of the concept and the varying levels of geopolitical tension each country has with China (Gewirtz, 2023). Consequently, for MNCs, it is crucial to possess comprehensive knowledge in two key areas related to China: a deep understanding of current policies governing foreign businesses and entities in China and a thorough comprehension of consumer cohorts in the Chinese market.

This book delves into both aspects, with a particular focus on comprehending the evolving landscape of consumer nationalism in China and providing guidance on how MNCs can effectively manage their public relationships within the Chinese market. By gaining insights into the dynamic policies and consumer sentiments in China, MNCs can formulate robust "de-risking" strategies that align with the unique challenges and opportunities presented by this complex environment.

The central focus and argument of this book revolve around the increasing risk that nationalist consumer outrage poses to businesses in China and those engaged with the Chinese market. As China faces growing diplomatic challenges on the international stage, MNCs will need to navigate these complexities with heightened caution by implementing strategic communication and public relations plans. Existing academic works on consumer nationalism in China primarily explore two key aspects: the delicate balancing act it presents for China's leaders and how the discourse of national pride and dignity reflects the complex interplay of China's ambivalent relationships with certain countries. While previous publications have provided valuable insights into the concept of consumer nationalism, its processes, participants, and initiatives, they have often overlooked the crucial analysis of its consequences. Therefore, it is essential to comprehensively examine and analyze the consequences of consumer nationalism in a systematic manner to provide a deeper understanding of its implications for businesses operating in China or engaged with the Chinese market. By shedding light on these consequences, this book aims to equip MNCs with the knowledge and insights necessary to effectively navigate the challenges and capitalize on the opportunities presented by China's evolving consumer nationalism landscape.

This book is a pioneering academic work that delves into the systematic analysis of the consequences of consumer nationalism by examining relevant cases in China over the past five years. Its primary objective is to equip MNCs with practical strategies for effectively managing the risks associated with consumer nationalism. To illustrate the gravity of the situation, the first chapter of the book presents the compelling case of South Korea's Lotte Group and its tumultuous experience with consumer nationalism in China. Lotte had invested a substantial sum of over $6 billion in China since entering the market in 2004. However, in 2017, the company made the difficult decision to withdraw from the Chinese market due to its inability to recover from a crippling boycott triggered by China's discontent with the South Korean government's installation of the American anti-missile Terminal High Altitude Area Defense (THAAD) system (Woody, 2017).

The opening chapter of the book serves as a contextual framework, situating China's consumer nationalism within the broader global landscape. It sheds light on the current trajectory of nationalistic sentiments among Chinese consumers and seeks to examine the extent to which these sentiments are a natural evolution or influenced by state-driven initiatives or state media. By exploring the case of Lotte Group and its implications, this chapter aims to establish the key research questions that underpin the subsequent chapters of the book. It sets the stage for a comprehensive exploration of consumer nationalism in China and its multifaceted implications for MNCs. Through this detailed examination, the book endeavors to provide valuable insights and strategies for MNCs to navigate the complexities of consumer nationalism and safeguard their operations in China's dynamic market.

Background and Focus

Nationalism has experienced a resurgence and has been on the rise globally in recent years due to a combination of factors. While the reasons for the rise of nationalism are complex and multifaceted, a number of factors have been considered as contributing to the phenomenon. Economic insecurities play a significant role, as globalization has led to economic disruptions and inequalities within societies. Job losses, wage stagnation, and economic uncertainties create fertile ground for nationalist narratives that promise to protect domestic industries, secure jobs for nationals, and prioritize national economic interests (Orazi, 2022; Wang, 2021; Woods et al., 2020).

Reactions to globalization have also fueled nationalist sentiments. Globalization's interconnectedness and the perceived erosion of national sovereignty have sparked resistance in some quarters. Nationalism often arises as a response to the perceived loss of control over national affairs, particularly in the face of global institutions, trade agreements, or supernational organizations that some perceive as encroaching on national decision-making processes. Cultural anxieties and debates surrounding migrants and refugees are intertwined with the rise of nationalism. Rapid cultural changes and increased immigration can generate fears of cultural assimilation or loss of national identity. In response, nationalist ideologies offer a sense of belonging, cultural preservation, and protection of heritage, resonating with those who feel their cultural identity is threatened. Political opportunism and the use of populist rhetoric have also contributed to the rise of nationalism. Charismatic leaders often tap into populist narratives to mobilize support. They exploit existing grievances, polarize societal divisions, and present themselves as champions of the people against established elites. By portraying their nationalist agenda as the solution to societal problems, these leaders attract followers who are disillusioned with traditional politics and yearn for change.

Similar to nationalism in other parts of the world, Chinese nationalism is also shaped by its unique historical, cultural, and political context. While there are some similarities between Chinese nationalism and nationalism in other countries, Chinese nationalism places a strong emphasis on territorial integrity and the notion of national rejuvenation. The concept of the "Century of Humiliation" is central to Chinese nationalism, referring to the period of foreign encroachment, colonialism, and unequal treaties that China experienced in the nineteenth and early twentieth centuries. Chinese nationalism seeks to overcome this historical period and restore China's status as a great power, often emphasizing the reunification of territories. Nationalism has been viewed as the most widely shared value both in Chinese society and in the government two decades ago (Cabesten, 2005). Since 2012, China has made nationalism central to its governance, as the country's leaders seek to achieve a "rejuvenation of the Chinese nation" (Zaagman, 2019). China's rapid economic growth and transformation over the past few decades have fueled a sense of national pride and confidence. The government's emphasis on achieving national rejuvenation and becoming a global power further enhances nationalist sentiments, as citizens associate economic success with national strength and pride.

The phenomenon of consumer nationalism in China has experienced a significant surge in recent years, reaching unprecedented levels of intensity (Jiang, 2021). This surge can be attributed in part to the widespread availability and accessibility of social media platforms and the internet across the country. These digital platforms have become breeding grounds for the dissemination of nationalist sentiments, enabling individuals to express their views, share information, and engage in discussions that reinforce a collective sense of national identity. As such, online spaces have played a pivotal role in amplifying nationalist discourse and shaping the consumer behavior of Chinese citizens.

This book stands out as the first comprehensive academic work that systematically analyzes the various waves of consumer nationalism in China. It delves into the intricacies of this complex phenomenon, exploring the different types of nationalistic consumer actions that have emerged and evolved over time. Moreover, it places particular emphasis on the critical impact of the new wave of consumer nationalism, which has heightened the likelihood of a consumer base detaching from a specific product or brand due to both anticipated and unforeseen triggers. By shedding light on the nuances and consequences of consumer nationalism in China, this book seeks to provide valuable insights and strategic guidance for businesses operating in or entering the Chinese market. By understanding the dynamics of consumer nationalism and its potential effects on their products and brands, companies can better navigate the challenges and opportunities presented by this powerful force.

The manifestations of nationalist consumer outrage have presented an increasing risk for businesses operating in China or those engaged in Chinese markets. This book contends that as China faces growing complications in its diplomatic relations abroad and experiences shifts in the characteristics of its core consumer base, MNCs need to adopt a more cautious and prepared approach when navigating the intricacies of the world's second-largest economy.

Furthermore, this book aims to address certain gaps in the existing research on consumer nationalism in China. While established academic works have extensively explored topics such as the delicate balancing act for China's governing body and the interplay between national pride and the country's ambivalence toward certain nations, there remains a dearth of analysis regarding the consequences of consumer nationalism. It is imperative to examine these consequences systematically in order to develop practical and proactive strategies for managing risks. While previous publications have provided valuable insights into the concept of consumer nationalism, its processes, participants, and initiatives, a more comprehensive understanding of its consequences is needed to devise realistic and effective de-risking strategies.

By delving into the repercussions of nationalist consumer outrage, this book will equip MNCs with the knowledge and tools necessary to navigate this increasingly complex landscape. By analyzing the consequences of consumer nationalism in a systematic manner, businesses will be better equipped to develop both proactive and reactive de-risking strategies that effectively mitigate potential challenges and capitalize on opportunities in the Chinese market. Ultimately, this book seeks to bridge the gap between theory and practice, enabling companies to navigate the multifaceted realm of consumer nationalism in China with confidence and foresight.

State Influence and Consumer Autonomy

One of the key questions that has emerged in the study of Chinese nationalism is whether these nationalist activities are entirely orchestrated by the state or if they are hybrid occurrences, where government warnings or objections are met with genuine citizen outrage or anger. The reality is that it is a combination of both. Over the past decade, observations and research on the topic indicate that there are cases where nationalist sentiments are initiated by social media or grassroots movements and later endorsed or amplified by state media outlets such as China Central Television (CCTV) (Jiang, 2014).

In some instances, nationalist sentiments may emerge organically from public grievances or concerns, often shared and spread through social media platforms. These sentiments may range from issues related to territorial disputes, perceived disrespect toward Chinese culture, or controversies involving foreign entities. The state media, including CCTV, may then seize upon these sentiments and provide coverage or commentary that aligns with the government's narratives. This can serve to further amplify nationalist sentiments among the population.

However, it is important to note that the government also exercises a degree of influence over the nationalist discourse. State media closely monitors and acts in a timely manner, adjusting their messaging or calling for "rationality" when nationalist movements could potentially lead to open criticism or challenges to the government itself. This suggests a sophisticated approach to balancing the expression of nationalist sentiment with the maintenance of social stability and the preservation of the government's authority.

This research study of Chinese nationalism reveals a combination of both "top-down" and "bottom-up" dynamics. Nationalist activities in China can originate from grassroots movements or social media, but they can also be influenced and guided by state media. The interplay between these factors demonstrates a complex and nuanced relationship between the state, society, and individual expressions of nationalism.

The incident involving the BMW Mini ice-cream at the Shanghai Auto Show in April 2023 serves as a poignant example highlighting the volatile combination of factors at play in the realm of consumer nationalism (Koetse, 2023). What initially seemed like a minor occurrence quickly snowballed into a significant controversy, with BMW being accused of racism by enraged Chinese consumers. Allegations arose that BMW staff distributed ice creams exclusively to Westerners while refusing to offer them to Chinese attendees on the exhibition day. The situation took a dramatic turn when a short video capturing this incident surfaced on Weibo, China's influential social media platform for public opinion shaping and agenda-setting, rapidly going viral and igniting a wave of nationalist sentiments. This outrage culminated in acts of vandalism and the burning of BMW vehicles by fervent nationalists across China.

Interestingly, amid the escalating tensions, a voice advocating rationality emerged at a critical juncture. Hu Xijin, the former editor of *Global Times* and a prominent figure in shaping public opinion in China, called upon consumers to consider the broader implications and consequences of their actions. In a post on Weibo, Hu urged Chinese consumers to think beyond the immediate anger and consider the detrimental impact such acts of aggression could have on China's own interests. He emphasized the efforts made by the Shanghai Convention Center in organizing the exhibition and attracting globally renowned brands to participate. Hu cautioned against letting the flames of nationalism overburn, highlighting the potential harm it could inflict on the host venue and ultimately undermine China's own objectives (Wenxuecity, 2023).

This incident serves as a powerful illustration of the intricate dynamics between consumer nationalism, public opinion, and rationality. It underscores the need for MNCs operating in China to navigate these complexities with tact and strategic foresight. By studying such cases and understanding the nuances of consumer sentiment, businesses can develop strategies that not only address immediate concerns but also consider the broader implications for their operations in China. Recognizing the potential impact on the host nation and appealing to rationality may prove instrumental in managing and mitigating the risks associated with nationalist outbursts, ultimately contributing to more sustainable and fruitful engagements with the Chinese market.

The case of Ye Shiwen's doping suspicion at the 2012 London Olympics provides another notable example that exemplifies the combination of both "top-down" and "bottom-up" factors in the realm of consumer nationalism. Ye Shiwen, a Chinese athlete, achieved an extraordinary feat by winning the gold medal in the women's 400-meter individual medley, shattering the world record by a second. Notably, her final 50-meter freestyle time of 28.93 seconds was even faster than the time recorded by Ryan Lochte, the American winner of the men's event, who finished with 29.1 seconds (Ramzy, 2012).

In the aftermath of her remarkable performance, John Leonard, the executive director of the World Swimming Coaches Association, raised suspicions about Ye's achievement, deeming it "suspicious" in an interview with the *Guardian* (Ramzy, 2012).

Western media journalists also started questioning Ye's performance; for example, Rick Morrissey from *Chicago Sun-Times* wrote:

> For those who believe a person is innocent until proven guilty, good for you. But for we skeptics, the people who have seen athletes try to beat the system over and over again, it's impossible to look at Ye's performance Monday and not suspect that something is very, very wrong. (Morrissey 2012)

BBC's sport commentator Clair Bauldin even expressed her concern to the whole world at the scene.

The accusation has triggered an intense reaction in China, where the Olympics are closely monitored. China achieved the highest number of gold medals at the Beijing Games in 2008, serving as a source of national pride and symbolizing the nation's renewed strength. The leader of China's Olympic swimming team vehemently dismissed any insinuation that Ye might have utilized performance-enhancing drugs. On July 30, the alleged BBC's biased suspicion was first criticized by Chinese netizens on Sina Weibo and started gathering attention from netizens. By July 31, it had been reposted for more than 20,000 times on Sina Weibo, and on the next day, Chinese state media broadcast the story and questioned the Western media bias in the suspicion of Ye Shiwen doping. On August 6, the esteemed academic journal *Nature* issued an apology to Chinese swimmer Ye Shiwen for hosting a contentious article on its website that inadvertently conveyed the impression of endorsing accusations against her, particularly in relation to doping.

However, in the Anti-Carrefour 2008 case, when hundreds of protesters demonstrated outside stores belonging to French supermarket chain Carrefour in four cities in China, state broadcaster CCTV sent different messages to advocate for calmness and rationality. The trigger was that Carrefour became a target of Chinese anger, drawing an outpouring of nationalism and indignation, after the chaotic Olympic torch relay in Paris, which saw pro-Tibet protesters trying to snatch the flame away from a wheelchair-bound athlete Jin Jing (Blanchard, 2008).

State broadcaster CCTV quoted an unnamed official from the Ministry of Commerce as saying that 99 percent of Carrefour's 40,000 employees in China are Chinese, and 95 percent of the products it sells are made in China. Chinese Foreign Ministry Spokesman Liu Jianchao told Reuters in an interview in the same week that China did not hate France. Mr. Liu said, "From the Chinese people's point of view, there isn't any hostility or hatred toward the French people. Their biggest feeling is probably puzzlement: why did such things happen in Paris?" (Blanchard, 2008).

One might ask why the Chinese government stepped in to support Carrefour during nationalist protests. Several reasons can be summarized to provide insights into this decision. First, it is considered extremely important to maintain social stability and avoid protests on the streets that could disrupt public order and create potential domestic chaos. By addressing the nationalist sentiment surrounding Carrefour, the government seeks to prevent the escalation of public discontent and maintain social harmony.

Second, Carrefour's operations in China employ a significant number of Chinese workers, approximately 40,000 employees. Protecting the interests and livelihoods of Chinese citizens is an important consideration for the government, as any negative impact on Carrefour's business could potentially harm the Chinese workforce and create economic instability.

Third, there was no serious political dispute or ongoing tensions between China and France during the time of the protests. The Chinese government's response to the nationalist actions surrounding Carrefour can be seen as a way to preserve diplomatic relations and avoid further strain on bilateral ties. It demonstrates a pragmatic approach to maintain a stable international environment while responding to domestic sentiments.

Therefore, interpreting consumer nationalist actions in China as solely "top-down" or "bottom-up" would be an oversimplification. Most cases involve complex interactions between state-led efforts, societal dynamics, and individual perceptions. The government's response to the Carrefour protests reflects a combination of factors, including the desire for social stability, the protection of domestic interests, and the management of international relations.

Case Study of Lotte

The Lotte Group, a South Korean company, has experienced one of the most severe consequences in recent memory. In 2017, South Korea entered into an agreement with the United States to deploy the THAAD system, an American anti-missile system, on its territory. This decision raised significant concerns in China, as there were worries that THAAD could serve as a spying tool, crossing a red line for Chinese authorities.

The initial repercussions of this situation were evident when concerts by Korean pop stars were canceled in Shanghai. However, tensions escalated further in March 2017 when Lotte, a South Korean company, provided land specifically for the construction of the THAAD system by the South Korean military.

Lotte had established a successful and influential market presence in China, operating over 112 supermarkets across multiple cities. Unfortunately, due to the THAAD controversy, the local governments ordered the closure of most of these supermarkets, citing violations of fire safety codes and other legal issues. Consequently, Lotte was compelled to sell all its supermarkets, leaving the company with only 13 cinemas and 2 department stores in China. As a result, Lotte, once a Fortune 500 company, lost its core business operations in China.

Apart from explicit policy and regulation-oriented actions, Chinese consumers also boycotted Korean cars, cosmetics, and snacks manufactured by Korean companies such as Orion. But there were exceptions. It is arguable that products that were at a higher level of the supply chain and vital for certain goods made in China were not subjected to these actions, such as Samsung's chipsets. The consequences of THAAD were significant as well as long-lasting. Although significant consumer boycotts against Korean products haven't been happening again, impacts on tourism and Korean TV and film are still effective. According to the statistics by the Hyundai Research Institute, South Korea suffered an economic loss of $7.3 billion as a result of the THAAD crisis, which is equivalent to half a percent of South Korea's GDP (Pak, 2020).

Through thorough case studies of consumer nationalism in China in the last five years, it becomes evident that the consequences of Chinese consumers' nationalistic actions toward certain brands can vary significantly. These consequences can have a profound impact on companies operating in the Chinese market. As such, it becomes crucial for these companies to gain a thorough understanding of the factors that trigger such actions and the potential outcomes they may face. By doing so, companies can proactively prepare strategies to navigate and mitigate the severity of these situations.

When it comes to understanding the timing and occurrence of these outcomes, companies should closely monitor the sociopolitical landscape and keep a finger on the pulse of public sentiment. This entails paying attention to potential flashpoints such as territorial disputes, historical grievances, or cultural sensitivities that may trigger nationalist sentiments among Chinese consumers. By staying well-informed and vigilant, companies can be better prepared to anticipate and respond to potential challenges.

Additionally, it is essential for companies to develop proactive measures to reduce the level of seriousness when confronted with nationalist actions. This requires adopting strategies that demonstrate sensitivity to local concerns, cultural values, and national pride. Companies should invest in building strong relationships with local stakeholders, including government authorities, community leaders, and influencers who can help navigate potential challenges.

Furthermore, companies should prioritize transparent and open communication with their Chinese consumers. Establishing clear channels for dialogue and actively addressing concerns can help defuse tensions and showcase a commitment to understanding and respecting local perspectives. By demonstrating a willingness to listen and adapt, companies can potentially alleviate the severity of nationalist reactions.

Therefore, understanding the potential consequences of Chinese consumers' nationalistic actions and developing strategies to navigate and mitigate them is vital for companies operating in the Chinese market. By proactively monitoring the sociopolitical landscape, building strong relationships, and engaging in transparent communication, companies can enhance their resilience and minimize the impact of nationalist sentiments. Ultimately, this approach can contribute to maintaining positive brand reputation, sustaining customer loyalty, and fostering long-term success in China's dynamic marketplace. This book aims to tackle these issues through a pragmatic approach with featured case studies.

Organization of the Book

Chapter 1 serves as an introductory chapter that lays out the central focus and argument of the book. It begins by presenting the case of South Korea's Lotte Group in China, which stands as a striking example of a company that has faced severe consequences. Lotte, having invested a staggering sum of over $6 billion in China since its entry into the country in 2004, recently made the announcement of its withdrawal from the market. This decision came as a result of the company's inability to recover from a debilitating boycott that emerged from China's dissatisfaction with the South Korean government's choice to deploy the American anti-missile system, THAAD. Within the context of China's consumer nationalism, Chapter 1 situates the phenomenon within a broader global landscape. It focuses on the current development of nationalistic sentiments among Chinese consumers and aims to explore the extent to which these sentiments are a "natural evolution" or are initiated and influenced by the state or state media. To illustrate the key research questions addressed in the book, the case of Lotte is introduced in this opening chapter, highlighting the complex dynamics between consumer nationalism, government actions, and the consequences faced by MNCs. Through the examination of this case, the chapter sets the stage for a deeper exploration of the intertwined factors shaping consumer nationalism in China and their implications for businesses operating in the country.

Chapter 2 delves into the notion that the pursuit of buying and personal pleasure has become a prevalent aspect of modern life in China. The advent and widespread popularity of social media video channels, such as Douyin, Redbook (Xiao Hongshu), Billibilli, and WeChat video channels, have played a significant role in reinforcing this trend in recent years. Collectively, these platforms have effectively amplified the theme of consumerism as economic individualism within Chinese society. The chapter argues that Chinese citizens have become self-managing consumers, actively engaging with and embracing consumer values as a defining characteristic of China's modern culture. By examining various nationalistic behaviors exhibited by Chinese citizens, Chapter 2 seeks to shed light on the intricate relationship between nationalism and consumerism in China. It tackles the question of how nationalism becomes embedded within the consumerist mindset of Chinese society. Through an analysis of consumer behaviors, preferences, and the cultural significance attached to consumption patterns, this chapter aims to provide insights into the interplay between nationalism and consumerism, illustrating how these two forces intertwine and shape contemporary Chinese society. By unraveling the dynamics between nationalism and consumerism, the chapter aims to contribute to a deeper understanding of the complexities involved in the expression of consumer nationalism in China.

Chapter 3 delves into the historical context of Chinese consumers' nationalism, exploring the distinct characteristics of each wave that has emerged over time. By taking readers on a journey through different periods, this chapter provides a comprehensive understanding of the evolution of consumer nationalism in China. It begins by recounting the well-known story of "The Shop of the Lin Family," a notable incident that exemplifies the eruption of nationalistic consumer boycotts in China in 1932. From there, the chapter traverses through significant events and shifts in public sentiment, ultimately reaching the more recent wave of public anger directed at South Korea, particularly targeting Lotte Mart in Beijing's Wanjing district in 2017. In addition to narrating the historical developments, Chapter 3 seeks to answer critical questions surrounding the evolution of consumer nationalism in China. It examines how consumer nationalism has transformed in recent years, identifying the key factors and societal changes that have shaped its trajectory. Furthermore, the chapter investigates the role of the government and state media in each wave of consumer nationalism, providing insights into their influence, interventions, and responses. By analyzing the consequences that have emerged from these various waves, the chapter sheds light on the potential outcomes and implications of the newly emerging wave of consumer nationalism in China. By exploring the historical context and its implications, Chapter 3 contributes to a comprehensive understanding of the multifaceted nature of consumer nationalism in China.

Chapter 4 sheds light on a crucial issue concerning existing studies on nationalism in China: the tendency to analyze Chinese nationalistic sentiments holistically, which, while informative, oversimplifies the complexities at play. The chapter argues that motivations behind nationalistic actions vary significantly among individuals and groups, necessitating a more nuanced approach to understanding consumer nationalism in China. To address this, the chapter advocates for the categorization of consumer nationalism into different types, based on a range of indices. By examining diverse types of consumer nationalistic actions in China and their respective consequences through illustrative cases, this chapter aims to provide a more comprehensive understanding of the multifaceted nature of consumer nationalism. It contends that consumer nationalism in China today can be classified into three distinct types, each engendering different levels of consequences. By dissecting these categories, the chapter not only deepens our understanding of the complexities of consumer nationalism but also highlights the varying impacts that different types of nationalistic actions can have on businesses, society, and the overall national discourse. Chapter 4 emphasizes the significance of recognizing the diversity within consumer nationalism in China, enabling researchers and practitioners to develop a more nuanced understanding of its manifestations and effects. By categorizing and exploring the different types of consumer nationalism, this chapter contributes to a more comprehensive framework for studying and addressing the complexities of nationalist sentiments in the context of consumer behavior in China.

Chapter 5 delves into the political implications of China's rise as the world's second-largest economy, which presents a complex landscape for multinational businesses. Drawing from the author's firsthand experience in training multinational firms operating in China, this chapter highlights the growing phenomenon of nationalistic outrage directed toward foreign brands. This outrage, fueled by real or perceived offenses to China and the Chinese people, has reached a fever pitch in recent years. After briefly introducing current key policies governing foreign businesses in China, this chapter emphasizes that this surge in nationalistic sentiment poses significant challenges for MNCs, both foreign and domestic, that are associated with certain foreign brands. As a result, these firms have become increasingly cautious when navigating the intricate dynamics of the world's second-largest economy. The pressure faced by companies operating in China is multifaceted, stemming from the country's more nationalistic stance and the increasing inclination to tighten governance and exert a direct role in business operations. By examining the political dimensions of China's economic ascent, Chapter 5 underscores the need for multinational businesses to carefully navigate the landscape of nationalistic sentiments. It emphasizes the importance of understanding and addressing the concerns of Chinese consumers and society, while also ensuring compliance with local regulations and cultural sensitivities. Through its analysis of the current business climate, this chapter provides valuable insights for companies operating in China, urging them to adopt strategies that balance economic objectives with the realities of an increasingly nationalistic environment. Chapter 5 serves as a reminder that China's economic prominence brings with it political implications that cannot be ignored by multinational businesses. By acknowledging and adapting to the heightened nationalism, companies can better position themselves to succeed in the Chinese market while fostering a mutually beneficial relationship with the country and its people.

Chapter 6 adopts a practical approach, examining the management of risks in the "new era" for businesses operating in China. As risks are constantly evolving in response to the larger environment, the nature of risks faced by companies in China has undergone significant changes in the past decade. Unfortunately, many foreign companies find themselves ill-prepared to effectively manage these evolving risks, increasing the likelihood of encountering unforeseen challenges. In 2017, China declared the arrival of a new era (xin shi dai), characterized by consumption-led growth, innovation, and a commitment to territorial integrity while taking a leading role in solving global challenges. The implications of this new era have a profound impact on foreign companies operating in China. Among the various risks that arise, heightened national pride, economic nationalism, and occasional anti-foreign sentiments pose the most significant challenges. In this chapter, an overall risk management plan is outlined, focusing on addressing the unique risks associated with China's new era. Special attention is given to discussing major instances of consumer nationalistic actions that have occurred in China over the past five years. Drawing on these case studies, the chapter proposes a range of pragmatic strategies that could have been adopted by companies to better manage risks in the face of nationalist sentiments. The chapter recognizes the critical importance for businesses to be proactive and adaptive in their risk management approaches in the Chinese market. By understanding and effectively addressing the challenges posed by heightened national pride and economic nationalism, companies can minimize potential disruptions to their operations and maintain positive relationships with Chinese consumers. The proposed strategies aim to strike a balance between risk mitigation and continued business growth, empowering companies to navigate the evolving landscape of nationalistic sentiments in China's "new era" successfully. Ultimately, Chapter 6 provides practical insights and actionable recommendations for businesses operating in China, enabling them to enhance their risk management capabilities and thrive in the dynamic and sometimes challenging business environment shaped by China's new era and its associated nationalistic sentiments.

Chapter 7 contextualizes the discussions in the book within a broader framework. It acknowledges the significant rise of nationalism in recent years, with the COVID-19 pandemic further accelerating this trend. The global response to the pandemic, including actions such as border shutdowns, fierce competition for medical supplies, and mutual blame for the origins of the disease, has propelled the wave of nationalism to new heights on a global scale. The increased geopolitical uncertainty and the prevailing social unrest witnessed worldwide indicate that these challenges are likely to persist. Policymakers and business operators find themselves grappling with the multifaceted implications of nationalism in both domestic and international contexts. This chapter delves into the broader challenges posed by the rise of nationalism, focusing on how it intersects with government intervention in markets and the potential threats it poses to the global economic system. The resurgence of nationalism has reshaped the global economic landscape, with governments asserting their influence over markets and placing greater emphasis on national interests. This shift introduces complexities for businesses operating in an interconnected world, as they must navigate a landscape where nationalistic sentiments and protectionist measures can impact their operations, supply chains, and market access. By examining the challenges presented by nationalism, policymakers and business leaders can gain a deeper understanding of the risks and opportunities associated with this phenomenon. They can explore strategies to address the tensions between nationalist agendas and the need for international cooperation and open markets. The chapter emphasizes the importance of fostering dialogue and collaboration among nations, promoting fair and transparent trade practices, and safeguarding the principles of the global economic system. Ultimately, Chapter 7 underscores the significance of the rise of nationalism and its intersection with government intervention in markets. It highlights the potential consequences for the global economic order and emphasizes the need for proactive and cooperative approaches to address these challenges. By recognizing the complexities and potential threats posed by nationalism, policymakers and business operators can work toward fostering a more stable and inclusive global economic system that balances national interests with the benefits of international cooperation.

Chapter 2

CONSUMERISM AND MODERN CHINA

Consumerism has undeniably emerged as a prominent aspect of contemporary Chinese society, permeating various facets of modern life. The proliferation and immense popularity of social media video channels such as Douyin, Billibilli, and WeChat have played a pivotal role in reinforcing and amplifying this consumerist trend in recent years. This phenomenon has been ideologically labeled as "consumerism as economic individualism," signifying the intertwining of consumerism with notions of personal economic pursuits and individual aspirations.

Chinese citizens have noticeably embraced the role of self-managing consumers, adopting consumer values as a defining characteristic of China's modern culture. The pursuit of material goods, lifestyle upgrades, and the constant pursuit of the latest trends have become deeply ingrained in the mindset of Chinese consumers. This conspicuous manifestation of consumerism has not only transformed the economic landscape but has also brought about profound social and cultural changes. Within this context, it becomes imperative to explore the relationship between consumerism and nationalism in China.

This chapter focuses on the examination of nationalistic behaviors exhibited by Chinese citizens, shedding light on how consumerism intertwines with and shapes nationalist sentiments. By delving into the intricacies of the younger consumer base and scrutinizing their evolving consumer preferences, this chapter seeks to answer the compelling question: How is nationalism embedded in consumerism in China? Understanding the complex dynamics between consumerism and nationalism is crucial for comprehending the broader sociocultural and economic landscape in China. By unraveling the interplay between these two powerful forces, we can gain valuable insights into the multifaceted nature of Chinese society and its ever-evolving relationship with consumerism, ultimately shedding light on the intricate tapestry of modern Chinese culture.

Consumerism in China (from Big Three to Luxury)

Consumerism, as a phenomenon, extends far beyond the borders of any single country. Nevertheless, it is in China that the scale and rapidity of its development have made it a remarkable case study for exploring the history and dynamics of this universal trend (Gerth, 2015). The embrace of consumerist values has sparked passionate debates, with proponents highlighting its ability to empower individuals by providing a means of self-expression through consumption—an attribute scholars often refer to as "agency." On the other hand, critics of consumerism argue that it fosters a narcissistic culture, placing excessive emphasis on material possessions and superficial desires.

In his comprehensive examination of consumerism's evolution in contemporary China, Gerth (2015) asserts that the history of the country since the Communist Revolution in 1949 reveals the pervasive influence of consumerist values across various socioeconomic systems, be they labeled as "capitalist" or "socialist." This observation implies that consumerism had already taken root in China long before the revolution, challenging the notion that it was solely a product of post-revolutionary reforms. Interestingly, consumerism in China and throughout the Communist Bloc was rarely wholly condemned or discredited. Even in the face of explicit state attempts to curtail or restrict it, earlier forms of consumerism, including the adoption of branded products and the associated identities they conveyed, managed to persist. Surprisingly, at times, state support was even extended to these consumerist endeavors.

The complex interplay between consumerism and state influence in China underscores the intricacies of its historical and cultural context. By recognizing the nuanced nature of consumerism's presence throughout Chinese history, we gain valuable insights into the multifaceted relationships between the individual, society, and the state. It is within this context that the exploration of China's consumerist journey yields rich findings and contributes to our broader understanding of this global phenomenon.

Gerth's (2020) insights shed light on the notable tension between consumerism and non-materialistic values that became increasingly apparent in contemporary China. This tension can be attributed to several factors, including China's relatively late start in the process of industrialization and the government's assertion that the nation was pursuing industrialization on a socialist path, rather than succumbing to "bourgeois" consumerism. This ideological stance set the stage for a complex interplay between the desire for economic progress and the preservation of non-materialistic values. China's drive to rapidly "catch up" with dominant global powers has yielded both positive and negative outcomes. On the positive side, China's remarkable economic growth and development have played a significant role in reducing extreme poverty on a global scale. In fact, close to three-quarters of the global reduction in the number of people living in extreme poverty can be attributed to China's efforts. This achievement underscores the transformative power of China's industrialization drive and its impact on improving the lives of millions of people.

However, the pursuit of rapid wealth accumulation and economic progress has not been without its challenges. The fervor to attain material prosperity has given rise to a host of associated issues. For instance, the relentless pursuit of wealth and economic success has led to growing income inequality, as disparities between the rich and the poor have widened. This wealth gap has raised concerns about social cohesion and fairness within Chinese society. Furthermore, the swift pace of industrialization and urbanization has exerted significant pressure on the environment, resulting in considerable ecological harm and pollution. The repercussions of this unchecked growth are apparent in challenges like air pollution, water scarcity, and the depletion of natural resources. These environmental issues not only jeopardize public health but also raise lasting sustainability concerns. The dual nature of China's speed to achieve economic prosperity highlights the complexities and trade-offs inherent in the process of industrialization. While it has undeniably brought substantial benefits in terms of poverty reduction and economic growth, it has also engendered a range of social, economic, and environmental challenges.

Phase 1: Three great things (Sandajian)

The initial phase of consumerism in contemporary China is exemplified by the concept of the "Three Great Things" or "sandajian" in Mandarin. This term refers to the three significant items that were highly coveted by marrying couples during specific time periods. In the 1970s, the Three Great Things encompassed a bicycle, watch, and sewing machine, representing symbols of progress and modernity for Chinese households. However, as China underwent economic reforms and opened up to the world, the composition of the Three Great Things evolved. By the 1980s, it had transformed to include a refrigerator, color television, and washing machine (Xinhua, 2021).

The expansion of the "sandajian" concept mirrors the changing aspirations and consumer preferences of the Chinese population. As China's economic development progressed, the range and significance of consumer desires extended beyond basic necessities to include a broader array of goods and services. This shift marked a turning point in the country's consumer culture and laid the foundation for the rapid growth and diversification of the Chinese consumer market. The recent emergence of the first China International Consumer Expo, held in Hainan Province in 2021, further illustrates the evolution of consumer behavior in China. This expo attracted over 1,500 companies from approximately 70 countries and regions, showcasing and trading high-end consumer products. The event showcased how consumption patterns in China have undergone significant transformations, with prosperity and abundance now reaching unimaginable levels for those who lived in China during the 1970s.

The China International Consumer Expo serves as a powerful symbol of the country's remarkable economic progress and the newfound purchasing power of its citizens. It highlights the nation's transition from a predominantly agrarian society to one characterized by a burgeoning consumer culture. The expo not only demonstrates China's growing influence as a consumer market but also signifies its integration into the global economy, as companies from around the world seek to tap into this vast consumer base. It is arguable that the evolution of the "sandajian" concept and the establishment of events like the China International Consumer Expo reflect the dynamic nature of consumerism in China. They provide tangible evidence of how consumption patterns have transformed over time, signaling a shift toward more diversified and sophisticated consumer preferences. As China continues to undergo economic growth and societal changes, the landscape of consumerism will undoubtedly continue to evolve, presenting new opportunities and challenges for both domestic and international businesses.

It is important to highlight that a prevailing notion in the People's Republic of China (PRC) was the aspiration to construct a society that was explicitly anti-capitalist and anti-consumerist. However, despite the Communist Party of China (CPC) coming into power in 1949, decades of mass campaigns and state propaganda denouncing "bourgeois" consumer desires as detrimental to the progress of "socialist construction" did not succeed in eradicating consumerism. In fact, these efforts inadvertently contributed to the further dissemination of consumerism into new social classes and regions (Gerth, 2015).

The existence and persistence of consumerism in China, despite the dominant anti-consumerist narrative, reflect the intricate and complex dynamics between the state and individual aspirations. While the government aimed to cultivate a society focused on collective progress and the fulfillment of basic needs, the allure of consumerism proved to be a powerful force that resisted complete suppression. State-led campaigns aimed at discouraging consumer desires often fueled curiosity and desire for the very goods and lifestyles they sought to discourage. Rather than extinguishing consumerism, these campaigns unintentionally helped create a demand for consumer products and fostered a consumer culture that transcended socioeconomic boundaries. As consumerism found new footholds in different classes and regions, it brought about social and cultural shifts, challenging the traditional notions of socialist construction and reshaping the fabric of Chinese society.

The endurance of consumerism in the face of state opposition speaks to the complexity of human desires and the intrinsic allure of material possessions. It also underscores the inherent tension between state ideology and the innate human inclination to seek out personal satisfaction and self-expression through consumption. The spread of consumerism into new classes and places suggests that individual aspirations and desires cannot be easily stifled by top-down directives, and they often find alternative routes for expression and fulfillment. The coexistence of consumerism and socialist ideals in China has generated a multifaceted society, where elements of both coalesce and intersect. This tension between consumerism and socialist principles continues to shape China's cultural landscape, as individuals navigate the space between personal desires and collective goals. Understanding this intricate interplay between consumerism and state ideology is crucial for comprehending the complexities of modern Chinese society and the evolving dynamics between individuals and the state.

The underlying reason behind the spread of consumerism in China extends beyond the influence of the state. While the government played a significant role in shaping consumerism, it was the general population who actively contributed to its dissemination by transforming once-unthinkable luxuries into everyday commodities (Gerth, 2015). This phenomenon is exemplified by the three most coveted products during the Mao era, which exemplify the role of mass production in propagating consumer values within a "socialist" country. The specific trio of highly sought-after products varied depending on the time period and location. In the 1970s, wristwatches, bicycles, and sewing machines held great allure, symbolizing progress and modernity. By the 1980s, color televisions, refrigerators, and washing machines became the coveted possessions, reflecting the changing aspirations and desires of the Chinese population. As the 1990s dawned, telephones, computers, and air conditioners emerged as new symbols of status and consumerism. By the 2000s, passenger cars, new apartments, and home theaters became the new benchmarks of success and prosperity (Qiu, 2010).

The evolution of these highly sought-after products illustrates the shifting priorities and expanding consumer landscape in China. What was once deemed a luxury or unattainable in earlier decades gradually became accessible and commonplace as mass production and economic reforms took hold. The desire for these items showcased the Chinese population's aspirations for improved living standards, increased convenience, and a higher quality of life. It is noteworthy that while the state initially aimed to discourage consumerism as a threat to socialist principles, the increasing availability and popularity of these everyday products inadvertently contributed to the spread of consumer values. Mass production and accessibility turned consumer goods into tangible symbols of progress, modernity, and social status, compelling individuals to embrace consumerist ideals.

The quest for these coveted items created a cultural shift and gradually ingrained consumer values into the fabric of Chinese society. As aspirations evolved, consumerism ceased to be a symbol of bourgeois influence alone but became a part of the broader societal fabric, shaping personal identities and influencing social dynamics. The ever-changing trio of coveted products reflects the dynamic nature of consumerism in China, driven by both societal and economic factors. Understanding the shifts in consumer preferences over time provides valuable insights into the evolving desires, aspirations, and values of the Chinese population, ultimately contributing to a deeper understanding of the complex relationship between consumerism, society, and the state in contemporary China.

The concept of the "Big Three" has experienced a gradual decline over the past decade, primarily due to the increased accessibility of global goods in China. As discussed above, the emergence of this concept can be attributed to the historical context of limited access to goods and merchandise in China until the 1970s. During the 1940s, many products were unavailable to ordinary consumers, primarily because they were either manufactured by foreign-owned companies or imported, making them unaffordable for the average citizen. The establishment of the PRC in 1949 brought about policies that aimed to address this scarcity and promote the acquisition of the "Big Three" items. These policies fostered a desire and pursuit of these goods among the Chinese population. Consequently, the concept of consumerism began to take shape during this period, as the once elusive "Big Three" items became increasingly accessible to both urban and rural residents across China.

The transformation of these three scarce items into commonly purchasable goods over the course of several decades illustrates the expansion of consumerism during that period. As the availability of these items grew, consumerism gained momentum and became an integral part of the Chinese social fabric. The increasing ability of ordinary citizens to acquire these goods not only fulfilled practical needs but also served as symbols of progress and improved living standards. With globalization and the opening up of China's market, access to a wide range of global goods has become easier than ever before. This greater availability of international products has contributed to a diminishing emphasis on the specific trio of goods that once defined the concept of the "Big Three." As Chinese consumers have more choices and exposure to diverse consumer products, their preferences have diversified, and the focus has shifted away from a limited set of goods to a broader range of options.

The evolution of consumerism in China highlights the dynamic nature of societal aspirations and the influence of economic factors on consumer behavior. The transition from a scarcity-driven consumer culture to an era of abundance underscores the profound changes that have occurred in Chinese society over the years. As the Chinese market continues to evolve and global trends shape consumer preferences, understanding the shifts in consumer behavior and the factors driving them is essential for businesses and policy-makers alike.

As mentioned earlier, the Big Three items of the 1980s encompassed TVs, washing machines, electric fans, and portable cassette players. However, during the 1990s, this selection shifted to include mobile phones, microwave ovens, refrigerators, and personal computers. In the new millennium, the Big Three transformed once again, now comprising cars, apartments, leisure travel, and other high-value items. As Gerth aptly summarized, the expansion of consumerism during this time was not only indicative of increased material consumption but also reflected the emergence of new waves of economic growth in China (Gerth, 2015).

To summarize, the growing demand for these consumer goods was spurred by the industrialization of China, which led to cost reductions and increased affordability. Labor-saving technologies, efficient transportation methods, and enhanced labor productivity (where the same amount of labor produced more goods) played crucial roles in making the Big Three more accessible to the general population (*Hangzhou Daily*, 1957a). In essence, consumerism, defined as the desire to express one's identity through the consumption or use of material possessions, gained traction among ordinary consumers due to the immediate practical benefits these items offered, as well as their social value within society.

Phase 2: Self-employed businesses (Getihu)

In 1978, China embarked on a transformative period known as "market reforms and opening," orchestrated by Deng Xiaoping, often referred to as China's "grand engineer" (Zhou, 1996). This era marked a significant turning point in Chinese society, and it was during this period that consumerism experienced substantial growth. A primary catalyst for this expansion was the rise of "Getihu," self-employed sole-trading businesses, which emerged because of top-level policy changes. There were a mere 150,000 private businesses in China at that time. However, within a decade, the number of Getihu skyrocketed to over 14 million (Young, 1995). This remarkable surge in entrepreneurial ventures was fueled by the relaxation of regulations surrounding small private plots for agricultural production and the establishment of small-scale private enterprises, which had been permitted since the 1970s (McEwen, 1994; Gold, 1991). As a result, millions of farmers gained access to increased disposable income, enabling them to participate in consumerism and fulfill their newfound desires.

The Getihu businesses encompassed a wide range of industries and services, covering everything from local dumpling stalls to interprovincial agricultural produce transport. Their presence was ubiquitous, permeating various sectors of the economy and offering diverse products and services to meet the growing demands of consumers. The proliferation of Getihu businesses played a pivotal role in expanding consumerism in China. These enterprises not only provided a means for individuals to pursue entrepreneurial endeavors but also contributed to the diversification and availability of consumer goods and services. With the newfound economic opportunities and increased purchasing power, Chinese citizens were able to embrace consumerism more extensively, further fueling the expansion of the market.

The rise of Getihu businesses and their significant impact on consumerism in China exemplify the profound changes brought about by the market reforms and opening policies. This period marked a departure from the previously centralized economic system, allowing for greater private initiative and entrepreneurial activity. The resulting surge in consumerism not only transformed the economic landscape but also reshaped social norms and aspirations, as individuals had access to a wider array of goods and services, enhancing their quality of life and opening new avenues for self-expression and personal fulfillment.

It is noteworthy to observe the shift in mindset regarding the obsession with foreign consumer goods. During the Mao era, wealth was often viewed as a potential crime against the state and indicative of "thought problems." However, with the introduction of Deng Xiaoping's new policies, particularly the official recognition and regulation of sole-trading businesses, there was a significant increase in the number of Getihu enterprises (Bruun, 1991). This marked a pivotal moment in the changing economic landscape of China. The rapid privatization of the economy led to the emergence of new social classes that enjoyed relatively higher levels of affordability and had greater demands for foreign consumer goods. The fast-growing speed of the economy created new opportunities for individuals to accumulate wealth and pursue their aspirations. As a result, the desire for foreign consumer goods became more prevalent among these newly empowered classes.

The relaxation of restrictions on private enterprise and the embrace of market-oriented reforms brought about a gradual shift in attitudes toward wealth and consumerism. The focus began to shift from viewing material possessions as symbols of crime or thought problems to recognizing them as indicators of progress and personal achievement. This transformation in mindset accompanied the evolving socioeconomic landscape, where the pursuit of wealth and access to foreign consumer goods became increasingly acceptable and even desirable. The changing dynamics of the Chinese economy, coupled with the growing aspirations of the new classes, fostered a consumer culture that placed a greater emphasis on the acquisition of foreign goods. These products represented not only status symbols but also served as tangible manifestations of social mobility and connection to the global market. The transition from a mindset that vilified wealth and foreign consumer goods to a more open embrace of prosperity and material desires was a significant aspect of China's changing socioeconomic landscape. The official recognition of sole-trading businesses, the rapid growth of privatization, and the emergence of new social classes all contributed to the shift in attitudes toward wealth and consumerism. This transformation set the stage for the rise of a consumer culture that valued foreign goods and reflected the changing aspirations and priorities of the Chinese population.

The question that arises is whether the governing bodies in China, at various levels, supported Deng Xiaoping's policy changes. The answer is affirmative, as state support played a crucial role in the success of Getihu enterprises. It was not merely a passive allowance for some individuals to get rich first; rather, state representatives, including Deng himself, actively implemented policies and intervened in local disputes to ensure the prosperity of actual Getihu businesses (Gerth, 2020). This active involvement from the state indicates a significant shift in China's governance, transitioning from the state shouldering all responsibilities to allowing the market to assume its new role, facilitated by state support and guidance.

The supportive stance of the government at all levels was instrumental in fostering an environment conducive to the growth of Getihu enterprises. By actively implementing policies that promoted private entrepreneurship and intervening to resolve conflicts or challenges faced by these businesses, the state played a pivotal role in enabling their success. This demonstrated a departure from the previous centrally planned economy and a recognition of the importance of market forces in driving economic growth and development.

The shift in China's approach, where the state facilitates and empowers the market, signifies a changing dynamic in governance and economic management. The government's active involvement in supporting Getihu enterprises reflects its recognition of the crucial role that private businesses play in driving economic progress and meeting the evolving demands of Chinese society. By allowing the market to take on new responsibilities while providing guidance and support, the state has created an environment that encourages entrepreneurial activities and economic innovation.

This collaborative approach between the state and the market has yielded positive outcomes, leading to the rapid expansion of private enterprises, job creation, and increased economic prosperity. The success of Getihu enterprises stands as a testament to the effectiveness of this model, where the state's proactive involvement in supporting and regulating the market has facilitated the growth of a vibrant private sector and contributed to China's overall economic development. The governing bodies in China, across all levels, actively supported Deng Xiaoping's policy changes and the emergence of Getihu enterprises. Their intervention and implementation of supportive measures highlight a shift from a solely state-driven economy to a system where the state enables and guides the market. This collaborative approach has been crucial in fostering entrepreneurship, encouraging economic growth, and transforming China's socioeconomic landscape.

It is indeed crucial to highlight that the big shift from a state-controlled economy to a market-oriented one was facilitated by central planning. The role of the state cannot be understated in creating an environment conducive to the growth of private businesses. The policy changes implemented at the central level played a pivotal role in providing space and opportunities for private entrepreneurs. One significant policy change was the removal of the political label "capitalist" that had been attached to the activities of self-employed individuals during the socialist transformation of the previous decades. This move was significant as it destigmatized self-employed individuals and signaled a more welcoming attitude toward private business owners in China. The shift in labeling and recognition of self-employment as a legitimate economic activity demonstrated a departure from the past ideologies and a willingness to embrace market-oriented practices.

Formal legalization of "self-employment" occurred in the 1980s through the government's creation of a new category of business licensing known as "geti gong-shang hu" or simply "getihu," referring to self-employment entities in industry and commerce. This step provided a legal framework for the operation of private businesses and further bolstered their legitimacy in the eyes of the state and society. The constitutional codification of self-employment in 1982 solidified its recognition as a supplementary segment of China's socialist economy based on public ownership. The state's commitment to protecting the legal rights and interests of self-employed economic elements was explicitly stated, providing a sense of security and stability for private business owners. In August 1987, the State Council issued the Provisional Ordinance on the Administration of Self-Employed Individuals in Urban and Rural Industry and Commerce serving as the primary legal framework for regulating Getihu enterprises until April 2011 when it was replaced by the Ordinance on Urban and Rural Industrial and Commercial Self-Employment. These policy changes and legal provisions exemplify the state's active role in supporting and regulating the private sector. The central planning and legislative measures enacted by the government were instrumental in creating a favorable environment for private businesses to thrive, encouraging entrepreneurship and contributing to China's economic transformation.

In summary, the shift from a state-driven economy to a market-oriented one was made possible through central planning and deliberate policy changes. The destigmatization of self-employment, the formal recognition and legalization of Getihu enterprises, and the legal protections provided by the state were key factors in facilitating the growth of private businesses. The active involvement of the state in shaping the regulatory framework and providing support was crucial in fostering a conducive environment for the flourishing of the private sector in China.

Phase 3: The commercialization of "everything"

The transformation of China from 1976 to 1997 is indeed remarkable, as highlighted by Chao and Myers (1998). If someone who had visited China in 1976, the year of Mao Zedong's death, were to return in 1997, they would be astounded by the tremendous changes and ask themselves if it is indeed the same country they once knew. One significant aspect of this transformation can be attributed to the policy empowerment initiated by the State Council. Between 1997 and 2007, the council implemented four rounds of revisions to the 1995 guidelines on sectoral entry by foreign investors. With each round of revisions, greater space was provided for the inflow of foreign capital into the country. This opening up to foreign investment played a crucial role in fostering a dynamic and innovative Chinese society in 1997.

The late 1990s saw a significant improvement in the living conditions of millions of urban families in China. They now resided in new apartment buildings, held new jobs, and enjoyed higher disposable incomes than ever before. These economic advancements resulted in the emergence of numerous new shops and elegant department stores that offered a wide range of goods and services previously unavailable to the Chinese population. This period witnessed a flourishing consumer culture, with a diverse array of products and services becoming accessible to the general public. The availability of such goods and the increase in consumer spending contributed to the vibrancy and vitality of Chinese society during that time. The infusion of foreign capital, along with the resulting economic growth, had a profound impact on the daily lives of Chinese citizens, transforming the country into a thriving marketplace with a multitude of opportunities and choices.

The relaxation and removal of restrictions on foreign entry into various service sector activities, such as banking, wholesale, and professional services, marked a significant change in China's economic landscape. This shift became particularly prominent after China's accession to the World Trade Organization (WTO) in December 2001. As a concession for its WTO membership, China opened up its market further, allowing greater participation of foreign businesses in previously restricted sectors. This policy change facilitated the entry of foreign-owned enterprises and promoted competition and innovation within these industries.

Another notable aspect of the revisions made to foreign investment guidelines was the gradual expansion of sectors where wholly foreign-owned enterprises were permitted to operate. This expansion created new avenues for foreign businesses to establish a presence in China and engage in various economic activities. The increased presence of foreign companies in China not only stimulated economic growth but also brought with it new technologies, management practices, and market dynamics, contributing to the overall development of the consumer market. In addition to policy changes, the influx of rural migrants seeking employment opportunities played a crucial role in fueling the growth of consumerism in China. These individuals, driven by the aspiration to improve their economic conditions and embrace a better lifestyle, migrated to urban areas in search of job opportunities and a chance to fulfill their desires. The aspirations and dreams of these migrants, coupled with their willingness to work hard and earn money, added to the momentum of consumerism in China during that time.

The shift from a collective-centered individual in 1976 to an autonomous consumer in 1997 was a significant societal transformation. The urban individual of 1997 was motivated by new appetites and dreams, driven by a desire to enhance their quality of life. The prevailing question in the minds of many was, "How can I acquire more money to afford the goods and services that will bring greater pleasure and meaning to my life?" This shift in mindset reflected the changing values and aspirations of Chinese society as it embraced consumerism as a means of personal fulfillment and self-expression.

Consumerism has undergone a significant transformation in China since the 1990s. This shift can be attributed to China's economic liberalization, which involved the development of private businesses, the attraction of foreign investment, and the subsequent privatization of state-owned enterprises (Hye-Jin Paek and Zhongdang Pan, 2004). Remarkably, the Gross Domestic Product per capita tripled in 1997 compared to the figures from 1978 (Fang, 2022). As a result, people's lifestyles have undergone substantial changes, and a thriving consumer market for goods and new merchandise has emerged. Li (1998) aptly summarizes this shift, stating that the Chinese, once indoctrinated with the belief that "consumption" was a symbol of decadent bourgeois influences, now find themselves surrounded not only by an increasing abundance of consumer goods and services but also by a deluge of promotional messages and activities.

According to Jiang's observations in 2012, being a consumer held significant value among Chinese internet users during the early 2000s. This sentiment was actively encouraged by Chinese internet companies, as highlighted in a Morgan Stanley analysis from 2005. The analysis suggests that Chinese internet companies emphasizing consumer value have the greatest potential for generating shareholder value. It is important not to underestimate China's dominant position as the world's leader in mobile subscribers and internet users under the age of 30, as emphasized in the Morgan Stanley report.

The cultural diffusion of consumerism is a widespread phenomenon globally, as noted by Qiu in 2003. However, the embrace of consumerism by Chinese netizens is particularly remarkable. The Norton Online Living report (2009) conducted a comprehensive survey across 12 countries, including the United States, Canada, the United Kingdom, France, Germany, Italy, Sweden, Japan, India, Australia, Brazil, and China. The survey, which examined online habits of approximately 9,000 adults and children, inquired whether participants spent more than an hour a month on the internet. This comparative study, at the time of writing, revealed that consumer behavior strongly reflects individuals' valuation of internet resources, and it also highlighted distinct cultural preferences and variations in online behavior between countries such as China and the United States, which possess the largest online populations.

The survey results indicate that, in general, the Chinese population demonstrates a greater propensity than Americans to adopt new technologies. A significant 82 percent of Chinese internet users surveyed engage with social networking sites, compared to only 47 percent in the United States. Additionally, 54 percent of Chinese respondents play online games frequently or consistently, contrasting with 27 percent in the United States. Moreover, a staggering 56 percent of Chinese individuals surveyed spend a minimum of 10 hours per month online, which is more than 9 times the 6 percent of internet users in the United States. The emergence of a consumer culture within Chinese cyberspace is astonishing yet comprehensible when viewed in the context of China's evolving landscape. China, once burdened by poverty and Communist ideology, has undergone a profound transformation and has become inundated with consumerist ideals. It is noteworthy that an iPod Nano in China costs US$179.84, exceeding the average monthly income of many individuals. Nevertheless, the prevalence of white earphones in the country remains conspicuous (French 2007). For those Chinese individuals earning approximately US$1000 per month, spending 80 percent of their salary on a Louis Vuitton key ring is not an uncommon occurrence (QQ News 2008). Instances of showcasing luxury purchases and flaunting wealth through personal blogs are abundant (Netease News 2008).

The concept of consumerism was not originally native to China, and what sets China apart is the stark contrast in ideology that prevailed before its introduction. The nation and its people underwent a significant shift from a mindset of enduring hardship during the 1970s and 1980s to one focused on pursuing pleasure (Qiu, 2010). Consequently, this transition to hedonism has fostered a widespread enthusiasm for online consumption among Chinese citizens. The desire to make purchases and indulge in personal gratification has become a defining characteristic of modern life in China. In recent years, the rise in popularity of social media video channels like Douyin, Billibilli, and WeChat has further amplified this narrative, effectively reinforcing the trend of consumerism among the Chinese population.

Consumerism and Nationalism

Promotion of consumerism

Recent literature suggests that the Chinese government endorses the frustration expressed by Chinese netizens toward Western media. In return for loyalty to the state, the government indirectly or overtly supports consumerism as a legitimate form of freedom for its citizens. Chinese Generation Y, in particular, has come to value the increased social freedom offered by shopping and internet communication, surpassing what was available to earlier generations. This newfound freedom has played a crucial role in fostering the loyalty of this generation toward the Chinese state.

From 1989 to early 2000, a consistent theme in displays of Chinese nationalism and loyalty has been a disapproval of Western ideology (Gries, 2004; Zheng, 1999). However, from early 2000 till several years ago, Chinese online users have showcased a new attitude characterized by a willingness to consume Western cultural products while harboring resentment toward Western political ideology. Despite an increasing number of Chinese individuals consuming Western goods like Starbucks coffee, wearing Adidas shoes, obtaining Western degrees, and even becoming permanent residents of Western countries, their love for their homeland, China, continues to grow stronger. While love for one's motherland is not unique to China, among the Chinese population, it predominantly serves as an expression of support for the central government.

Strategic use of government power

Examining the Chinese government's management strategies can provide insights into how the Chinese people perceive their nation. Utilizing a Foucauldian analysis, for instance, reveals the intertwined nature of nationalism and political power, forming inseparable bonds. Political movements aiming to attain state power often legitimize their actions through nationalist arguments (Breuilly, 1993, p. 1). Some regard nationalism as inherently political (e.g., Brass, 1991), capable of transforming political landscapes (Hobsbawm, 1983). Anderson (1991) proposes a close analytical connection between nationalism and ethnicity, referring to contrasting chains of connections called "serialities" (p. 11), which can be either bound or unbound. However, governmental roles play a crucial role in any examination of modern nationalism, and "bound" chains established by the government can foster a sense of community, influencing the development and politics of ethnic identity. Anderson further argues in his study of Indonesia in "Imagined Communities" that nationalism is often aligned with "large cultural systems that precede it," such as religious communities and dynastic realms (Anderson, 1991, p. 12). Although the case of Indonesia differs from that of China in several aspects, Anderson's methodology, which involves analyzing print media, maps, census surveys, and museums, illustrates how focusing on governmental techniques can aid in understanding the underlying forces and influences of nationalism.

Foucault's concept of governmentality encompasses a similar theme to Anderson's analysis. Foucault posits that any examination of nationalism inevitably falls within the framework of governmentality. In his analysis of power relations and government processes, he depicts societies as operating through two potentially conflicting games: the citizen game and the shepherd-flock game (1988, p. 71). The interplay between these games often shapes the narrative of the modern state. Foucault's identification of pastoral and sovereign power aligns with Anderson's analysis of large cultural systems. Eudaily (2004) suggests that such configurations offer unique analytical tools (p. 40). Therefore, given the significance of Foucault's analysis and the related approaches mentioned above, it is worth exploring the meaning of pastoral and sovereign powers. According to Foucault, sovereign power pertains to the legal enforcement of citizen responsibilities (see Dean, 1991), usually centralized and repressive, with laws derived from royal rule. Consequently, a diagram of sovereign power positions the sovereign head outside the political system (Eudaily, 2004, p. 39). On the other hand, pastoral power connects individual needs, state obligations, and societal well-being, focusing on personal moral salvation (Dean, 1991, pp. 81–2). Unlike centralized sovereign

power that operates in a top-down manner, pastoral power employs personal-
ized strategies aimed at producing individual effects, valuing the well-being
of a single person as much as that of the entire community (Foucault, 1983,
p. 219). Diagrams of pastoral power thus place a moral and reflective ethos at
the core of a state. Foucault refers to the tactical exercise of power by institutions as the "art of governmentality" (Foucault, 1991, p. 3).

According to numerous analysts, there exists a strong connection between
nationalism and governmentality. In the context of this study, adopting
Foucault's concepts of pastoral power and sovereign power allows us to
observe a notable shift in the exercise of governmental power in China, enabling Chinese younger generations to shape their unique brand of nationalism. In Foucauldian terms, the Chinese government has transitioned from
the use of sovereign power to the application of pastoral power.

Generation Y's nationalistic perspective

The emergence of a new wave of nationalistic sentiment presents a striking
contrast to earlier aspirations for progress toward an open and democratic
society in China, as evident among Generation Y. This generation displays
minimal interest in acquiring greater political power. Furthermore, the historical context reveals an intriguing relationship between democracy and
nationalism in China. Following Deng Xiaoping's post-1976 modernization program, Chinese nationalism took on a pro-Western stance as rapid
economic development prompted intellectuals to advocate for democracy.
However, after the 1989 democratic movement failed, Chinese nationalists
swiftly began questioning the influence of Western culture in China. They
positioned themselves as realistic and pragmatic defenders of stability and
order. While this generation of nationalists did not bring about democracy in
China, the desire for it still lingered. Nonetheless, the new wave of Chinese
nationalism embodied by Generation Y, born after 1980, marks a notable
shift. The complex interplay between Chinese nationalism and democracy
is not a novel topic. Scholars since the 1990s have highlighted the tendency
of nationalistic sentiment in China to clash with democratic aspirations, particularly in disputes concerning national boundaries. While earlier analyses
post-Mao mostly assumed Chinese citizens' yearning for democracy and
acknowledged the democratic potential of nationalism (He, 2003; Wang,
2003), the current wave of Chinese nationalism demonstrated by Generation
Y appears to contradict these previously optimistic viewpoints. In essence,
this latest wave of Chinese nationalism is characterized by resistance to structural change. The post-1980 generation in China is the first to grow up in
a consumerist society with access to the internet, and many of these young

individuals are pampered as single children. The ongoing reforms and opening up have satisfied their curiosity about the world, and Western influences, such as Coca-Cola, Hollywood movies, and iPods, are ingrained in their everyday lives. Consequently, they exhibit little interest in engaging in political transformations. For them, as prosperity and personal freedom are attainable, democracy is deemed unnecessary. A member of Generation Y encapsulates their sentiment as follows: "Our life is pretty good. I care about my rights when it comes to the quality of a waitress in a restaurant or a product I buy. When it comes to democracy and all that, well [...] [that] doesn't play a role in my life" (Elegant, 2007).

But to what extent is Generation Y's nationalistic sentiment and resentment toward the West free of the government's intervention or influence? As the earlier analysis has already intimated, to assume that it is free of it would be to oversimplify the reality. Accordingly, I propose that China's Generation Y's nationalistic sentiments are stimulated through the government's promotion of the online consumer culture.

The interpretation of Chinese nationalism

The issue of comprehending Chinese nationalism is further complicated by the ongoing debate surrounding the role of the Chinese government in shaping it (Zhao, 2004, pp. 12–14). Scholars hold differing perspectives on whether Chinese nationalism emerges organically from the grassroots or is imposed from the top-down by the state to serve the interests of the Communist Party (CCP).

The prevailing Western perception tends to view Chinese nationalism as a construct of the ruling elite, representing the interests of the Communist state. According to this view, nationalism serves as a means of safeguarding the state from foreign influences. This perspective asserts that the Chinese lack an inspired version of nationalism founded on shared ideals and noble principles. Instead, their nationalism is characterized by a strong sense of "us versus them," often fostering xenophobic sentiments (Pye, 1996, p. 67). The state exercises its authority to enforce nationalism through various means, thereby playing a pivotal role in constructing and managing national identity dynamics (Dittmer and Kim, 1993, p. 87). Outside China, perceptions of Chinese nationalism are influenced by alternative understandings of international relations (Zheng, 1999, pp. 4–5). Specifically, in the West, two prominent theories—realism and liberalism—have shaped how the international implications of Chinese nationalism are perceived. From a realist standpoint, China's nationalism emerged as a consequence of the post-Cold War era, creating a "power vacuum" in East Asia that allowed ethnic tensions to resurface (Buzan and Segal, 1994, p. 15). China, bolstered by its rapid economic growth and modern development, sought to fill this void (Zheng, 1999, p. 5), which generated palpable anxiety regarding the potential for conflicts with neighboring countries (Kristof, 1993; Roy, 1995, pp. 48–50). On the other hand, liberals contend that while war is unlikely among democratic states, the remarkable economic progress of China poses a clear threat to its neighbors (Doyle, 1983; Owen, 1994; Russett, 1993). Liberals also argue that there exist fundamental disparities in how peace is experienced in Europe versus Asia. Most European states are stable democracies with relatively low levels of social and economic differentiation, a circumstance that is less prevalent in Asia. Furthermore, regimes in the Asian region exhibit considerable variation, ranging from totalitarian North Korea to a mix of modernizing and authoritarian governments in Southeast Asian countries, and the distinct form of capitalism in China (Friedberg, 1993/4, pp. 5–33).

Liberals further assert that China's advancing nuclear capability poses a significant threat to global peace (Buzan and Segal, 1994; Segal, 1995; Roy, 1995). While realists and liberals propose different approaches to address China's ascent as a global power, they concur on the role played by the CCP in fostering Chinese nationalism. The prevailing Western interpretation of Chinese nationalism maintains that "the Communist Party has deliberately cultivated Chinese nationalism as a means to legitimize its own rule" (Gries, 2004, p. 18). In response, realists argue for the need to constrain China's nationalism and balance its power. They advocate for measures aimed at limiting China's economic development as a way to weaken its influence (Segal, 1995, p. 73). On the other hand, liberals believe that with continued economic and cultural progress, China will inevitably transition to democracy. Drawing from the experiences of political development in other East Asian nations, they contend that sustaining economic growth while maintaining political monopoly is an increasingly untenable balancing act, especially in an interconnected world driven by communication and trade. As people's incomes rise and their horizons expand, the demand for participatory governance and protection under the rule of law becomes more pronounced (Talbot, 1996, p. 57).

However, both liberals and realists share the belief that the CCP has strategically fueled nationalism as a means to maintain its grip on power during political crises. Some have even argued that "the Chinese Communist Party is no longer purely communist [...] [and] must emphasize its Chinese identity even more" (Christensen, 1996, p. 38). In essence, as the ideological influence of communism has weakened, nationalism has gained even greater significance as a tool for the government. Consequently, there exists a broad consensus in the West that contemporary Chinese nationalism serves as a crucial propaganda tool employed by the Communist regime to consolidate its authority (Gries, 2004, p. 18).

Thus, the prevailing Western perspective on the recent hostility displayed by Chinese bloggers toward news that is clearly critical of China is that it stems from Communist indoctrination. While this perception holds some truth, I believe it oversimplifies the complexities of Chinese nationalism.

The dominant Chinese perception: "Bottom up"

According to the "bottom-up" view, Chinese nationalism is eternal and objective; it reflects the people's attitudes rather than the government's interests (Gries, 2004; Zheng, 1999). Three clear reasons why Chinese nationalism reflects popular rather than government interest have been proposed: First, it is about how the Chinese state should and can be reconstructed in accordance with the changing domestic and international circumstances. Second, it is about state sovereignty and people's perception of China's proper position of power in a world of nation-states. Third, it is about people's perceptions of a "just world order," an international system that accords with China's national interest (Zheng, 1999, p. 14). In other words, Chinese nationalism is not simply party propaganda because Chinese citizens now play a central role in how nationalism is conceived and developed. The Chinese, like all peoples, "have deep-seated emotional attachments to their national identity" (Gries, 2004, p. 18, one of very few Western scholars to comment on the link between emotion and nationalism).

Overseas Chinese scholars also argue that the role of the CCP is less influential than is commonly thought (Fong, 2004; Zhao, 2002; Zhou, 2005b). The basis for their argument is that although most overseas Chinese have access to different information and therefore are free from Chinese state intervention, there is no evidence that liberalism, for example, is more popular than nationalism among them. In 2003 and 2004, the anthropologist Vanessa Fong conducted research among young Chinese adults studying in Australia, Ireland, the United Kingdom, and the United States. Her findings indicate that despite daily exposure to everyday life in the West and Western media perspectives, students expressed a nationalistic Chinese attitude when interviewed about the 1999 bombing of the Chinese embassy in Belgrade (Fong, 2004). Her findings echo those of mainland Chinese research, for example, that of sociologist Zhao Dingxin. After interviewing over 1,200 elite university students in Beijing, he claimed that exposure to Western media sources had little effect on young people's degrees of anger regarding the embassy bombing (Zhao, 2002). I am myself one of China's Generation Y and living overseas with the opportunity to closely observe the young generation's lifestyle at home and abroad, I agree that liberalism does not appear to be more popular than nationalism among young Chinese. Since the reasons for this are not clearly understood, they are worth deeper consideration. It is arguable that this phenomenon has been neglected in studies of nationalism among China's young generations, and further, that an explanation may be found through studying the Chinese state's tactics of governmentality, that is, why the government chooses to encourage some forms of self-sufficiency and independence ("technologies of the self" in Foucault's terms) rather than employ the machinery of propaganda.

Bridging the difference

It is possible to claim that the consequences of the Cultural Revolution and the Tiananmen Square incident caused Chinese Generation Y's current apathy to democracy, so that there was no need for the CCP to seek to influence young people's attitudes to it. When Generation Y's parents talk about the chaos of the Cultural Revolution, the stories their children hear may be sufficient to make them apolitical. Most parents warn their children never to join alternative political movements in China. In any case, regardless of such advice, the chapter on political unrest and confrontation in Chinese history is ancient history to most of the young generation. What Generation Y has witnessed and experienced with its own eyes are a peaceful China and the country's economic boom. Some members of Generation Y have vague memories of the Tiananmen Square protest in 1989, but they tend to believe that such protests are no longer needed and would actually be counter-productive: If popular uprisings like Tiananmen were allowed to continue, they would have provoked a counteraction by conservative forces and led to a return to fortress China: no more overseas shopping trips or snowboarding weekends (Elegant, 2007).

The preference for consuming certain Western products over democracy also raises something else worthy of consideration: Among this internet-savvy, pragmatic younger generation, how could nationalistic sentiment be formed by external factors if it is not also their natural emotion? And if it was formed by external factors, for what purposes? It is certainly not simply party propaganda from the top anymore, because the CCP does not openly talk about nationalism. In fact, the Chinese government is cautious about evoking nationalistic sentiment because it is aware that Chinese nationalism is a double-edged sword that could one day turn against the government itself, as it did in demonstrations against the American government embassy in 1999, and the Japanese government embassy in 2004 when violent protests by aggressive Chinese anti-Japanese demonstrators erupted on the streets of

Shanghai and dozens of other Chinese cities for several days (Zhao, 2005). Hence, the Chinese government knows that nationalism poses a potential threat to the current political framework. This may explain why in the case of anti-CNN protests in 2008 there were no street demonstrations in domestic China at all. The anti-CNN case, a clinching episode for the argument of this book, is analyzed in Chapter 6. But to explain nationalism as arising solely out of an emotion from below that comes from the Chinese people themselves is also too simple.

The CCP does have a nationalist strategy, but it is more sophisticated than previously acknowledged. The CCP has awoken nationalistic sentiments through promoting a consumerist culture, and it is this strategy that has enabled it to penetrate to the roots of Chinese consciousness. By encouraging the pursuit of personal economic freedom as an ultimate goal, nationalism is stimulated at the same time. This effect is particularly evident in Chinese cyberspace, where much consumerist activity and social interaction now occurs. In this sphere, political strategies can be waged more subtly than in any direct state or policing interventions. Thus, nationalism can be engendered by the state through a complex range of strategies, an array of "technologies" connecting the strategic calculations of the political center and a state's institutions to thousands of micro-locales where individual or group conduct is shaped (Rose, 1999b, pp. xxi–xxii).

"Guo Chao (National Trend)" in China

Recent research conducted by New Zealand Trade & Enterprise has shed light on a concerning trend: trust in products from Western countries has been on the decline in China, leading to a shift in consumer preferences toward domestic brands. This finding has gained further traction with an increasing number of media reports and academic observations highlighting the same phenomenon (Jiang, 2021). Against a backdrop of growing national pride and frequent boycott actions directed at international brands across various sectors, Chinese domestic brands are experiencing remarkable sales growth.

According to recent data, the first three-quarters of 2020 witnessed a 2 percent increase in domestic sales for Chinese fast-moving consumer goods brands, while foreign brands experienced a significant 6 percent decline year-on-year. Multinational companies and marketing firms operating in the PRC have observed a distinct shift in the behavior of young Chinese consumers, who are displaying a heightened sense of nationalism and a propensity to favor domestic brands over their foreign counterparts (Jiang, 2021).

This emerging trend reflects a deeper sentiment among the younger generation in China, who are increasingly aligning their purchasing decisions with their national identity and demonstrating a stronger preference for products that are seen as homegrown. As China's economic and technological advancements continue to gain global recognition, coupled with a renewed sense of national confidence, young Chinese consumers are embracing domestic brands as symbols of national pride and quality (Yang, 2021; Yu and Wu, 2021).

The implications of this shift in consumer behavior are significant not only for international brands but also for the broader dynamics of the global market. As Chinese consumers increasingly embrace domestic products, multinational companies will need to navigate a more complex landscape to maintain their market share and appeal. Understanding and effectively responding to the evolving nationalist sentiments and preferences of Chinese consumers will be crucial for brands seeking success in this dynamic and rapidly changing market.

Credit Suisse's annual surveys on emerging consumers have provided insightful findings since 2018, indicating a noticeable increase in national pride among Generation Z in the PRC (Credit Suisse, 2018). Analysts from the financial services firm have observed that improvements in product quality, marketing strategies, and distribution, coupled with a growing skepticism toward imported products, have contributed to a greater confidence in domestic brands in recent years (Credit Suisse, 2021). Moreover, the COVID-19 pandemic and geopolitical tensions have acted as catalysts, further propelling the demand for homegrown brands in China. Consequently, domestic brands are positioned to thrive in the market. This survey has also revealed that more than 90 percent of young Chinese consumers aged 18 to 29 expressed a preference for purchasing domestic home appliance brands in the coming 6 to 12 months.

A stark contrast in attitudes toward foreign brands can be observed when comparing Generation Z to the preceding generation, known as "Generation Y." In a highly influential book titled *Cyber-nationalism in China*, which extensively explores Generation Y's perspective on the West and remains a prominent reference in the field of Chinese nationalism, the wave of nationalism among Generation Y was described as characterized by paradoxical sentiments toward the West. They were found to embrace Western culture and consume Western brands while harboring deep resentments toward Western ideology.

However, the dynamics have shifted significantly. The present wave of Chinese nationalism exhibits distinct characteristics. While the resentment toward Western ideology remains, if not intensified, China is witnessing the emergence of a consumer generation that is increasingly inclined to choose domestic brands, fueled by a burgeoning sense of national pride. Nevertheless, attributing these new attitudes solely to national pride would be an oversimplification. Other factors and complexities contribute to this evolving consumer behavior.

Conclusion

This chapter serves as a comprehensive exploration of the nationalistic behaviors exhibited by Chinese citizens, while also delving into the shifts occurring within the younger consumer base. Its primary objective is to address the question of how nationalism intertwines with consumerism in China. Building upon these insights, the subsequent chapter endeavors to offer a systematic examination of the evolving attitudes toward foreign brands among China's emerging consumer cohort. By carefully dissecting the underlying elements beneath the nationalistic undertones, this book stands as a pioneering work in academia, being the first to thoroughly analyze the distinct characteristics of China's new wave of consumer nationalism in a holistic manner. Through this comprehensive approach, a deeper understanding of the complex relationship between consumerism and nationalism in China is elucidated, providing valuable insights into this dynamic and evolving landscape.

Chapter 3

NATIONALISM AND THE GREAT REJUVENATION OF THE CHINESE NATION

This chapter aims to provide readers with a comprehensive historical context surrounding the phenomenon of Chinese consumers' nationalism, shedding light on the distinct characteristics exhibited by each wave throughout time. By delving into pivotal moments, such as the renowned narrative of "The Shop of the Lin Family," which vividly portrays the eruption of nationalistic consumer boycotts in China back in 1932, to the more recent events like the fervent public backlash against South Korea and its impact on Lotte Mart in Beijing's Wangjing district in 2017, this chapter offers a captivating journey through the evolution of consumer nationalism in the country.

Within the pages of this chapter, readers will find answers to pressing questions regarding the transformations witnessed in Chinese consumer nationalism in recent years. By examining the changing dynamics, it seeks to unravel the multifaceted nature of this phenomenon and explore the various factors that have contributed to its evolution. Specifically, the chapter endeavors to shed light on the role played by the government and state media in each wave, deciphering their influence and exploring their motivations. This chapter also contemplates the ramifications that may arise from the emergence of a new wave of consumer nationalism. By drawing upon historical insights and analyzing current trends, it endeavors to provide a forward-looking perspective on the potential consequences of this evolving phenomenon. As society navigates through this new wave, it becomes increasingly crucial to understand the implications it may have on various aspects, including politics, economics, and social cohesion.

Ultimately, this chapter serves as an invaluable resource for readers seeking to grasp the intricate tapestry of Chinese consumers' nationalism throughout history. By examining each wave's characteristics, unraveling the role of government and state media, and anticipating the potential outcomes of a burgeoning new wave, it invites readers to engage critically with this complex and ever-evolving aspect of Chinese society.

History of Chinese Consumers' Nationalism

Consumer nationalism emerged as a recurring theme in the dynamic relationship between China and the Western world, gaining notable prominence during the late nineteenth century and reaching its zenith between the 1900s and the 1940s. Throughout this period, several pivotal instances of consumer nationalist movements unfolded, leaving a lasting impact on Sino-Western relations. The first notable nationwide consumer nationalist action in China transpired in 1905, with a particular focus on American goods. This movement was fueled by a strong perception among Chinese citizens that their compatriots residing in the United States were subjected to harsh and unjust treatment. As a result, merchants in major Chinese cities took a unified stand, refusing to trade American products. This collective action sent a resounding message to both the American government and businesses, highlighting the dissatisfaction and grievances harbored by the Chinese populace. Another significant consumer nationalist movement occurred in 1925, this time targeting British goods. The catalyst for this action was the mounting outcry over Britain's diminishing political influence in China. As nationalist sentiments gained traction, Chinese consumers deliberately shifted their preferences away from British products, seeking to express their discontent and assert their national identity.

The 1930s witnessed a surge in anti-Japanese sentiment, leading to widespread rejection of Japanese goods. This wave of consumer nationalism was a response to Japan's expansionist ambitions and aggressive policies in China. Chinese citizens, driven by patriotic fervor and a desire to protect their national interests, actively boycotted Japanese products, effectively disrupting Japan's economic influence within the country. Throughout the early twentieth century, numerous smaller-scale antiforeign boycotts occurred, further illustrating the enduring presence of consumer nationalism in China. These localized actions were often triggered by specific events or grievances, and while not as widespread as the nationwide movements, they reflected the underlying sentiments of Chinese consumers, seeking to safeguard their national pride and economic interests. Collectively, these instances of consumer nationalist actions during the late nineteenth century and the first half of the twentieth century underscored the Chinese people's desire to assert themselves in the face of perceived injustices and encroachments by foreign powers. These movements represented a tangible expression of Chinese nationalism, where consumer choices became intertwined with political and social aspirations, providing a platform for citizens to voice their concerns and reshape the dynamics of Sino-Western relations.

A significant lens through which to interpret these historical consumer nationalist behaviors is to recognize their role in raising awareness among Chinese consumers about the perception of being marginalized or mistreated by dominant global powers. These movements served as powerful vehicles for the Chinese populace to voice their frustrations and grievances, consequently fostering a heightened sense of national consciousness and unity. By actively participating in consumer nationalist actions, Chinese consumers found a tangible means to express their resentments and convey their dissatisfaction with the perceived bullying tactics employed by the great powers. These actions provided a platform for individuals to collectively assert their national pride and solidarity, transcending individual grievances to embody a broader sentiment of resistance against external pressures.

These consumer nationalist movements not only reflected the existing Chinese nationalism but also acted as catalysts, fueling its further development and momentum. The act of consciously boycotting foreign goods and favoring domestic alternatives became an embodiment of the Chinese people's determination to safeguard their national interests and preserve their cultural identity in the face of external influences. Through these actions, Chinese consumers were able to reshape their narrative, asserting their agency and challenging the dominance of foreign powers. As noted by Putten, these historical consumer nationalist behaviors were deeply intertwined with the broader fabric of Chinese nationalism. They served as both expressions of the collective aspirations of the Chinese people and catalysts for further mobilization and consolidation of nationalistic sentiments. The impact of these actions reverberated beyond the economic sphere, permeating various aspects of society and shaping the course of China's relationship with the outside world. In essence, the historical consumer nationalist movements in China were instrumental in raising awareness among Chinese consumers about their perceived mistreatment, serving as outlets for expressing their frustrations. These movements not only represented the collective will to resist external pressures but also played a crucial role in galvanizing and nurturing Chinese nationalism. By embracing and mobilizing consumer choices as a means of asserting their identity and protecting their interests, Chinese consumers forged a path toward empowerment and contributed to the ongoing evolution of the nation's collective consciousness.

The undercurrent of antiforeign nationalism, as observed in the historical consumer nationalist movements, laid the foundation for the establishment of political parties that played pivotal roles in China's history. The Chinese Nationalist Party, which held power until 1949, and the Chinese

Communist Party (CCP), which assumed power thereafter, both drew upon and harnessed the sentiments of this nationalism to shape their ideologies and agendas. Scholars have highlighted that the true concern in Chinese-Western relations, stemming from these nationalist movements, lies not solely in the immediate economic repercussions but rather in the potential political ramifications. The power of politically inspired popular movements cannot be underestimated, as they have the propensity to spiral beyond control or prediction. The implications extend beyond economic realms and can significantly impact the overall stability and dynamics of the relationship between China and the Western world.

As emphasized in the last chapter, to view these movements solely as top-down initiatives oversimplifies the complexity of nationalism as a force throughout history and on an international scale. Nationalism itself has consistently demonstrated a dual nature, serving as both a unifying force and a potential source of conflict. Its influence is multifaceted and often influenced by a variety of factors, including social, cultural, and historical contexts. While political actors and institutions may attempt to harness or manipulate nationalist sentiments for their own agendas, the underlying swell of nationalism originates from the collective consciousness of the people. It emerges from a deep-rooted sense of identity, pride, and the desire to protect national interests. Thus, to fully understand the motivations behind these actions, it is essential to recognize the intricate interplay between top-down influences and bottom-up popular sentiments.

The historical context of Chinese nationalism highlights the delicate balance and inherent complexities associated with this phenomenon. Nationalism can be a powerful force that unites people under a common cause, empowering them to resist perceived threats. However, it can also become a double-edged sword, leading to potential tensions and challenges in international relations. By acknowledging the multifaceted nature of nationalism and understanding its historical significance, we gain a more nuanced perspective on the dynamics of Chinese-Western relations. It becomes clear that navigating the impact of nationalist sentiments requires a comprehensive approach that considers both top-down policies and the grassroots origins of nationalistic movements. Recognizing the complexities at play enables a more informed and balanced analysis of the historical and contemporary dynamics between China and the Western world.

From Linjia Puzi (the Lin Family Shop) to Lotte—different waves

An exemplary case that epitomizes the intertwining of consumer culture and modern Chinese nationalism is that of Linjia Puzi. During the early twentieth century, a burgeoning consumer culture emerged, shaping and disseminating the ideals of modern Chinese nationalism. China witnessed a surge in the importation and local manufacturing of a myriad of consumer goods, transforming the everyday lives of millions of Chinese individuals who eagerly embraced, discussed, and aspired to these commodities. But alongside the rapid influx of imports and the desires they generated, concerns and anxieties arose among various segments of Chinese society. Politicians grew apprehensive about trade deficits and the emergence of new consumer lifestyles epitomized by opium dens and addiction. Intellectuals, who had begun engaging with Western political economy, expressed fears of losing sovereignty in the face of growing foreign dominance over the commercial economy. Manufacturers, faced with the competition of inexpensive and superior imported goods, grappled with the challenge of preserving or expanding their market shares.

Consequently, these multifaceted concerns gave rise to a nationalization of consumerism in China. Unlike the definition of consumerism in other countries, Chinese consumerism of that time emphasized the constraints placed on individuals rather than individual freedom. Consuming "national products" became a means for people to demonstrate their support for the nation, and the act of consumption itself became imbued with patriotic significance. Consequently, consumers were categorized as either patriotic or treasonous, depending on their choices and preferences (pp. 13–17). This convergence of consumer culture and nationalism in China during this era represents a distinct manifestation of the country's social and political landscape. The interplay between consumer desires, economic concerns, and national identity shaped the contours of Chinese society, as individuals were urged to align their consumption patterns with the nation's goals and aspirations. The idea of consuming "national products" went beyond personal satisfaction and became intertwined with a sense of duty and loyalty to the country. Understanding the nuances of this historical context enables a deeper appreciation of the complexities surrounding Chinese consumerism and nationalism. It illuminates how economic factors, political anxieties, and cultural expectations converged to shape consumption practices and define notions of patriotism. The Linjia Puzi example exemplifies the intricate relationship between consumer culture and nationalism, underscoring the ways in which consumption became a platform for both expressing and defining Chinese national identity.

"The Lin Family Shop" (1932), a poignant short story penned by the renowned Chinese writer Mao Dun (1896–1981), provides a compelling illustration of the nationalization of consumerism during that period. Set against the backdrop of Japan's escalating military aggression against China in 1931, the narrative captures the prevailing sentiments and struggles of the Chinese people. Amid the backdrop of Japan's aggressive expansionism, growing anger among the Chinese populace fueled a widespread boycott of Japanese goods. In the story, a privileged teenage girl, belonging to a modest merchant family, returns home from school in distress. Her classmates and teachers have subjected her to harassment due to her stylish new dress, which is crafted from Japanese fabric rather than Chinese material. While the girl is cognizant of the criticism leveled against her, she finds herself torn. On one hand, she understands the aggressive control Japan has been exerting over China, making the boycott of Japanese products an expected act of resistance. On the other hand, she cherishes her possessions, which include Japanese clothing, cosmetics, pencils, and even an umbrella. Despite her appreciation for these items, the mounting social pressure becomes unbearable.

The girl grapples with the conflict between her personal desires and the nationalist sentiments pervading society. Ultimately, to escape further torment and conform to the prevailing social expectations, she confronts her mother, demanding an immediate replacement of her wardrobe with garments made from Chinese fabrics. This story captures the complex emotions and dilemmas faced by individuals during a time of heightened nationalism. It portrays the tension between personal preferences and the collective call for patriotic actions. The girl's internal struggle reflects the broader societal pressure to align consumption choices with the nationalistic cause. Through the lens of "The Lin Family Shop," Mao Dun delves into the intricacies of consumer nationalism and the sacrifices individuals were expected to make in service of the nation. It highlights the deep emotional connection people had with their possessions, even when those possessions originated from the very source of national resentment. The story sheds light on the societal dynamics and the profound impact of nationalist sentiment on personal choices, further emphasizing the complexities and challenges inherent in the nationalization of consumerism during that era.

Within the broader context of the early nationalization of consumerism wave, the struggles faced by shop owners like Mr. Lin in selling imported Japanese merchandise were profound. In the case of Linjia Puzi, the fictional shop depicted in the story, the challenges and hardships endured by the protagonist and the dire circumstances surrounding his business become evident. As the movement to boycott Japanese goods gained momentum, feudal warlords saw an opportunity to exploit the situation. Under the guise of supporting the boycott, they resorted to extortion and coercion, demanding exorbitant sums of money from various shops, including Linjia Puzi, in the form of protection fees. These fees were essentially a form of extortion, forcing merchants to pay to continue their business operations without facing retribution.

Mr. Lin, the owner of the small shop in the Hangjiahu area of Jiangnan Province in 1931, found himself caught in the crossfire of turbulent times and economic depression. Despite his repeated struggles to navigate the challenging social and economic landscape, he was ultimately driven to bankruptcy under the relentless exploitation imposed by these dark forces. Through the lens of "Lin Jia Puzi," Mao Dun masterfully portrays the devastating consequences faced by shop owners like Mr. Lin. The story encapsulates the precarious position these merchants found themselves in during a period of political and economic turmoil. They not only contended with the pressures of conforming to the nationalistic boycott but also had to navigate the exploitative tactics employed by the very forces purportedly supporting the movement.

By highlighting the plight of Mr. Lin and the ultimate collapse of his business, Mao Dun sheds light on the broader systemic challenges faced by merchants during this era. The story underscores the vulnerability of small business owners in the face of political manipulation, economic hardships, and the consequences of nationalization efforts. The tale of Linjia Puzi serves as a sobering reminder of the personal tragedies and sacrifices that unfolded amid the nationalization of consumerism movement. It encapsulates the devastating impact that external pressures and exploitation can have on individuals, families, and businesses caught in the crosscurrents of political and economic forces. Through this narrative, Mao Dun exposes the harsh realities of this historical period, offering a poignant reflection on the complexities and repercussions of the early stages of consumer nationalism in China. The young woman's decision reveals the pervasive tensions between consumerism and nationalism that were, as Gerth (2003) argues, central to the creation of China as a modern nation. The sad outcome of Linjia Puzi shows that all industries are living in potential persecution when facing consumer nationalistic actions.

The establishment of the People's Republic of China in 1949 marked a significant turning point, bringing an end to the era of unrestricted consumer choice for Chinese citizens. Under Mao Zedong's regime, the focus shifted from consumer-oriented cities to transforming them into centers of production, mirroring the economic model of the Soviet Union that prioritized state-owned heavy industries rather than consumer goods. This shift resulted in the gradual expulsion of foreign multinational companies from China, leading to the disappearance of most foreign products from store shelves. There was a brief period of hesitation initially, allowing consumer lifestyles to persist until the mid-1950s. However, the state eventually took over all private enterprises, effectively outlawing consumer culture. For the next three decades, China underwent a significant transformation. Following Chairman Mao's death in 1976, Deng Xiaoping introduced economic reforms and implemented the Open Door Policy, which aimed to open China to foreign trade and investment. As a result, the importation of consumer goods was gradually permitted. Chinese policymakers recognized that allowing imports was a small price to pay in exchange for accessing foreign consumer markets for their own products.

As the range and quantity of imports have expanded, tensions between "Chinese products" and "foreign products" have periodically resurfaced in the last 30 years. One contributing factor is China's commitments as a member of the World Trade Organization (WTO), which have rendered numerous village-owned and state-owned enterprises unable to compete and resulted in the unemployment of millions of workers, causing frustration and resentment. Chinese students, in particular, continue to invoke the language of economic nationalism, advocating for boycotts of foreign goods. An example of this occurred during the widespread boycott of the French retail giant Carrefour in 2008 as a response to the disruption of the Olympic torch relay in Paris. These instances reflect the ongoing tensions and occasional re-emergence of economic nationalism in China, as various social and economic factors continue to shape consumer attitudes and behaviors. The journey of consumerism in China has been marked by shifts in government policies, economic reforms, and fluctuations in attitudes toward foreign products. From the initial restriction of consumer culture under Mao's regime to the subsequent opening up of markets and the occasional resurgence of economic nationalism, China's consumer landscape has witnessed significant transformations over the decades.

In the past century, China has made remarkable strides in establishing itself as a global manufacturing powerhouse. Its rapid industrialization and manufacturing capabilities have propelled the nation's economy to new heights. However, as the world shifts toward service-oriented economies in the so-called "post-industrial" era, Chinese leaders and businesses recognize the need for China to transition into a branding superpower. The Chinese government and business leaders have understood that in the modern global marketplace, the ownership of global brands and intellectual property holds significant symbolic value, representing national wealth and power. They aspire to see Chinese brands become globally recognized and respected, serving as ambassadors for the nation's capabilities and innovation.

To support the development of national brands, the Chinese government has implemented various initiatives and policies aimed at fostering innovation, protecting intellectual property rights, and encouraging entrepreneurship. Efforts are being made to enhance the overall quality and reputation of Chinese products and services, both domestically and internationally. These initiatives seek to bolster the competitiveness of Chinese companies in the global marketplace and establish a solid foundation for the growth of Chinese brands. While the progress may not have been as rapid as anticipated, Chinese companies are gradually gaining recognition and establishing their presence in global markets. With a concerted focus on quality, innovation, and effective brand management, Chinese brands have the potential to make a significant impact and achieve the desired goal of becoming globally recognized symbols of China's wealth and power.

Therefore, in modern China, consumers have a complex attitude toward foreign products. On the one hand, the patriotic spirit drives them to support national products. On the other hand, there are not enough national brands that have the same competitiveness as foreign brands. Therefore, they are still buying foreign products, but at the same time, hoping Chinese national products will develop further (Gerth, 2013). China's government is doing its best to support the development of China's brands and put some restrictions on foreign brands at the same time. The fierce competition with Chinese domestic companies also urges foreign companies to adapt themselves to China's market. For example, their Chinese names are expected to be connected with a good image in China, and their products must fit the preference of the Chinese (Gerth, 2013, pp. 115–21).

In this manner, Chinese consumers are not simply ceasing to purchase foreign products, but rather reevaluating them through a lens of nationalism. Before making a purchase, they assess the degree to which a foreign product can be considered "Chinese." This attitude represents a shift from the consumer behavior observed in the 1930s. During that time, the boycott of foreign products was primarily driven by "consumer ethnocentrism," which emphasized the avoidance of purchasing foreign goods due to concerns about harming the domestic economy and a sense of unpatriotic behavior (Shimp and Sharma, 1987, p. 280). In contrast, the contemporary attitude of Chinese consumers can be categorized as "consumer nationalism." This perspective emphasizes the notion of consumption as a political statement, involving both the deliberate avoidance of products from countries deemed offensive and the support for domestically produced goods and services (Gerth, 2011, p. 280).

The boycott directed at Lotte Mart serves as a prime example of the recent surge in consumer nationalism in China. The controversy emerged following the signing of a deal on February 28, 2017, which granted permission for the United States to construct an anti-missile system on land owned by Lotte, a South Korean firm. Lotte Group had been operating in the Chinese market since 1994, with major affiliates like Lotte Mart and Lotte Department Store entering through joint ventures. In 2012, the group established a new headquarters in Shanghai, comprising Lotte Shopping, Lotte Corp, and Lotte Chemical, and actively expanded its business operations in the Chinese market. The Chairman of Lotte Group, Shin Dong-bin, had set a sales target of 200 trillion won ($164 billion) for 2018, with China being a key strategic market. This instance highlights how consumer nationalism manifests in the form of boycotts, where Chinese consumers respond to perceived offenses by foreign companies or nations. The boycott against Lotte Mart exemplifies the mobilization of consumer sentiment to express displeasure and exert pressure on companies involved in politically sensitive issues. Such incidents underscore the role of consumers in shaping economic and political dynamics, as their actions reflect a fusion of personal consumption choices and nationalistic sentiments.

As introduced in Chapter 1, the retail conglomerate Lotte has seen its business shrinking in China and losing market share after the company in 2017 announced support for the Terminal High Altitude Area Defense (THAAD). China's government has responded by encouraging an outpouring of public anger directed not just at Lotte, whose shops in China were boycotted, but almost anything South Korean. Chinese consumers were furious at its decision to deploy the missile-defense system, known as THAAD (the first components of which arrived in South Korea on March 6th). Consumers refused to consume in Lotte Mart not just because it is a foreign company, but because they felt their nation was offended. Nationalism is already embedded in China's consuming culture and shows itself through consumers' behavior. After investing $9.6 billion, South Korea's Lotte exited the market in 2019.

Building upon Gerth's observations in 2013 that Chinese consumers have not completely stopped purchasing foreign products, it is important to note that the most recent wave of consumer nationalism in China has witnessed the emergence and increasing popularity of new Chinese brands. As illustrated in Chapter 2, these brands have gained significant traction and appeal among Chinese consumers, reflecting the evolving dynamics of consumer nationalism in the country. The next section of this analysis will delve deeper into each wave of nationalism in China, exploring the distinct characteristics and drivers behind each wave. By examining the historical context and understanding the underlying factors that shape consumer nationalism, we can gain insights into the current state of nationalism in China and its implications for domestic and international markets.

By tracing the historical progression of consumer nationalism, we can discern patterns and trends that have influenced Chinese consumers' preferences and behaviors. Understanding these patterns will shed light on the motivations and attitudes of Chinese consumers toward both domestic and foreign brands. Exploring the features of the current wave of consumer nationalism in China will provide valuable insights into the evolving landscape of the Chinese market. This examination will help identify the factors that contribute to the rise of new Chinese brands and their increasing popularity among consumers. It will also shed light on the role of government policies, social media, and cultural influences in shaping consumer nationalism in China. By delving into these aspects, we can gain a comprehensive understanding of the complex interplay between nationalism, consumer behavior, and market dynamics in China. This knowledge will serve as a foundation for developing effective strategies and approaches for businesses operating in the Chinese market, as well as for policymakers seeking to navigate the complexities of consumer nationalism in the country.

Features of the Current Wave of Nationalism

To gain a deeper understanding of the current wave of consumer nationalism in China, it is crucial to trace the roots of Chinese nationalism back to 1949 when the People's Republic of China was founded by the CCP. However, comprehensively analyzing Chinese nationalism from 1949 to 2021 is a challenging task within the scope of this overview. The complexity arises not only due to the ambiguous nature of nationalism itself but also because, as Wang Gungwu emphasizes, the study of Chinese nationalism encompasses multiple layers and facets (Wang, 1996, cited in Zheng, 1999, p. x). Considering the vastness and intricacies of Chinese nationalism, it is difficult to capture all its aspects in a single study. To address this challenge and ensure relevance to this particular research, Chinese nationalism from 1949 to the present can be divided into six distinct phases. The first phase, known as the Mao era, spans from the establishment of the People's Republic of China in 1949 until Mao Zedong's death. The second phase, covering the years from 1976 to 1989 (after Mao's death and before the Tiananmen Square incident), marked a period of political transition and economic reforms under Deng Xiaoping's leadership. The third phase, from 1989 to 2001 (after the Tiananmen Square incident and before China was elected to host the 2008 Olympics), witnessed both internal and external challenges for the Chinese government. The fourth phase, spanning from 2001 to 2008, coincided with China's preparation and hosting of the 2008 Beijing Olympics. The fifth phase, from 2008 to 2016, witnessed the launch of initiatives such as "Made in China 2025" that aimed to strengthen China's manufacturing capabilities and achieve technological self-sufficiency. Attitudes toward Western ideologies during this period reflected a determination to reduce reliance on foreign technology and foster indigenous innovation. The final phase, from 2016 to the present, has been marked by an assertive and self-assured China on the global stage. The attitudes toward the West have evolved, with Chinese nationalism taking on a more prominent role in shaping China's policies and international engagement.

Examining these different phases of Chinese nationalism provides valuable insights into the shifting attitudes and perceptions toward Western ideologies and the West itself. By understanding these dynamics, we can better comprehend the current wave of consumer nationalism in China and its implications for domestic and international affairs. The next section will explore characteristics of each phase, including the prevailing attitudes toward Western ideologies during that period and the Chinese perspective toward the West (see Table 3.1).

Phase 1

In 1949, the establishment of the People's Republic of China by the CCP was rooted in anti-Japanese sentiments, which laid the foundation for Chinese nationalism. During this period, Chinese nationalism was expressed through a "victor narrative," emphasizing heroic Chinese victories over Western and Japanese imperialism (Gries, 2005, p. 106). The CCP sought to shape a national identity by presenting the Soviet Union as an ideal model for the new Chinese nation (Wei, Liu, and Kirby, 2002, p. 83). Aligned with the Soviet Union's revolutionary path, the CCP adopted a Marxist-Leninist doctrine of nationalism, which viewed political behavior as driven by economic interests (Zheng, 1999, p. 69). Consequently, nationalism was often regarded as a form of "disguised economic interest" or, in Marxist terms, as "false consciousness" that diverted people from pursuing their true class interests (ibid.). China enthusiastically pursued close ties with the Soviet Union, making invitations to Soviet specialists a national policy and eagerly embracing Soviet influence across various administrative sectors (Wei, Liu, and Kirby, 2002, pp. 83–6). However, China soon realized that this close apprenticeship with the Soviet Union conflicted with its goal of building a strong and independent nation-state (ibid., pp. 90–4). This conflicting interest ultimately led to the end of China's honeymoon with the Soviet Union in 1960 (Zheng, 1999, p. 69). The concept of nationalism was gradually

Table 3.1 Six phases of nationalism in China.

Six Phases of Nationalism	Characteristics	Attitude toward the West
1949–1976	"Victor narrative" of heroic Chinese victories over Western and Japanese imperialism	anti
1976–1989	More tolerant of Western ideas, including Party members	pro
1989–2001	Nationalism was promoted as a dominant discourse in China	anti
2001–2008	Pride and anti-Westernization narrative strengthened	anti
2008–2016	Extreme embrace of Western culture on the one hand, sharp resentment of Western political ideologies	paradoxical
2016–current	The move toward more Chinese brand consumption	detaching

Source: Author's own compilation.

replaced with a strengthened focus on "patriotism" and the building of a strong Chinese nation that unified all Chinese people (Zheng, 1999, p. 70). During this period, the ideology of patriotism was interpreted as being anti-imperialist, anti-feudalist, anti-Confucianist, and anti-capitalist (Zhang, 2001, p. 264). While products from the Soviet Union were welcomed initially, access to foreign brands overall remained limited in China at that time. This historical context highlights the evolution of Chinese nationalism and the changing dynamics of China's relationship with foreign powers. From an initial emphasis on Soviet influence to a shift toward a stronger and more independent national identity, the early phases of Chinese nationalism set the stage for subsequent developments in consumer attitudes and the emergence of consumer nationalism in China.

Phase 2

After the death of Mao in 1976, Deng Xiaoping emerged as a key figure in Chinese politics and initiated a comprehensive modernization program with the goal of strengthening and enriching China. This marked a significant shift in Chinese nationalism toward pro-Western ideologies, setting the stage for a transformative period in the country's history. However, this phase of pro-Western sentiment and the aspirations for democracy were abruptly interrupted by the tragic events that unfolded during the 1989 Tiananmen movement. During this pivotal period leading up to the Tiananmen Square protests, China witnessed the exercise of what Michel Foucault termed "pastoral power." This form of power was intricately tied to the concept of the living individual and their needs, as highlighted by Dean (1991, p. 81). The

Chinese government, under Deng Xiaoping's leadership, sought to address the immediate needs of the people while simultaneously exerting control over political dissent.

The implementation of Deng Xiaoping's reform and opening policy in the 1980s brought about remarkable improvements in the living standards of the Chinese population. The rapid economic growth resulting from these reforms led to a significant rise in the overall well-being of the people (Zheng, 1999, p. 50). One tangible indicator of this progress was the substantial increase in the ownership of household color televisions, with the ratio skyrocketing from less than 1 percent to 70 percent between 1981 and 1991 (ibid.). Simultaneously, the spread of Western ideas, including the concept of "democracy," began to flourish within China. A nationwide survey conducted in 1987 revealed that a staggering 75 percent of Chinese citizens were tolerant of the influx of Western ideas, and even within the CCP, 80 percent of members held similar views (Min, 1989, p. 128). The rapid economic growth fueled by the reform and opening policy created an environment where the desire for democratization among Chinese intellectuals intensified. Many intellectuals believed that China's traditional culture was acting as an impediment to democratization, and they saw thorough westernization as the key to China's future.

The culmination of these aspirations for democracy and Western influence was exemplified by the construction of the "Goddess of Democracy" statue during the Beijing Spring of 1989. This iconic symbol, inspired by Western democratic ideals, represented the fervent desire of Chinese nationalists to promote the establishment of democracy in China (Gries, 2004, p. 6). However, the events that unfolded in Tiananmen Square in 1989, when the peaceful protests were met with a violent crackdown by the Chinese government, dramatically altered the trajectory of China's political landscape. The government's response effectively suppressed the pro-democracy movement, and the pursuit of Western ideals within China was severely curtailed.

Despite the setback experienced in the aftermath of Tiananmen, China's modernization and economic reforms continued to reshape the country in subsequent years. The economic growth propelled by Deng Xiaoping's policies not only improved living standards but also transformed China into a global economic powerhouse. China's approach to governance and nationalism underwent significant changes, adopting a more pragmatic and assertive stance on the international stage. This period between Mao's death in 1976 and the events of the Tiananmen Square protests in 1989 marked a complex and transformative phase in China's history. It was a time when the

Chinese government sought to modernize and strengthen the nation while grappling with the desires for democracy and westernization among its people. Ultimately, the tragic events at Tiananmen Square served as a turning point, altering the course of China's political development and shaping its trajectory in subsequent years.

Phase 3

The movement for democratization in 1989 ultimately did not succeed in achieving its goals. Chinese leaders, recognizing the potential destabilizing effects of political reform, focused on utilizing such reforms to strengthen and stabilize the Communist Party rather than weaken it (Zheng, 1999, p. 50). The aftermath of the Tiananmen Square protests witnessed a resurgence of sovereign power, as the government sought to reassert control and suppress dissenting voices. However, the sustained economic development that characterized the 1990s brought about a gradual satisfaction of individual needs among the Chinese population. As living standards improved and material aspirations were fulfilled, a complex interplay of top-down and bottom-up influences shaped Chinese nationalistic sentiments during this stage. Following the Tiananmen Incident in 1989, particularly with Jiang Zemin assuming power in 1992, nationalism began to be actively promoted as a dominant discourse in China. It was during this era that Chinese nationalism underwent a transformation, shifting from a more pro-Western sentiment to a more anti-Western stance (Zheng, 1999, p. 50).

Several factors contributed to the promotion of nationalism as a new ideology during this period. One significant influence was the collapse of European communism and the subsequent reflections on Western culture within China. The unraveling of communism in the Soviet Union and Eastern Europe prompted Chinese intellectuals to reevaluate traditional ideologies and consider alternative paths (Zheng, 1999, pp. 51–2). The changing nature of Chinese society also played a role in the emergence of nationalism as a dominant discourse. As China underwent rapid economic and social transformations, there was a growing sense of mismatch between the evolving society and the old ideological framework. This disparity further fueled the search for new ideas and identities, with nationalism emerging as a powerful force in shaping public sentiment (Zheng, 1999, pp. 51–2). The failure of the 1989 democratization movement led to a resurgence of sovereign power and a shift in Chinese nationalism. The sustained economic development of the 1990s improved living standards and fulfilled individual needs, while also contributing to the shaping of nationalistic sentiments. Influences such as the collapse of European communism and the changing Chinese society played crucial roles in the promotion of nationalism as a dominant ideology in China during this period.

Second, a notable shift occurred among Chinese intellectuals in their perception of the West. Prior to 1989, there was a belief that China needed to undergo comprehensive westernization. However, in the 1990s, the Western impact was increasingly viewed as "negative" and detrimental to Chinese traditional culture. Additionally, Chinese observers began questioning the intentions of the West in relation to China's rise, particularly when faced with stringent conditions imposed on China's entry into the WTO (Sun, 1996, p. 17).

Third, the old ideological framework in China had become outdated since the beginning of the reform and opening up in 1978. A new ideological tool was required to effectively manage the rapidly changing society, and nationalism emerged as the most suitable candidate (Chen, 1996, p. 74). Interestingly, Chinese nationalists during this phase embraced a narrative of "victimization" rooted in the "Century of Humiliation" (Gries, 2004, p. 4). They questioned the influx of Western culture that began flooding into China in the late 1990s. In 1997, Song Qiang, the author of the aforementioned 2009 nationalist book, "Unhappy China," reflected on the materialistic tendencies of his generation, lamenting the dominance of "cultural and spiritual fast food" (Song, 1997, cited in Gries, 2004, p. 4). This new generation perceived themselves as defenders of China's stability, viewing the previous generation before 1989 as dangerously romantic and radical (Gries, 2004, p. 5).

An illustrative example of this shift in nationalist sentiment can be seen in the "May 8th" nationalist protests of 1999. The demonstrations featured a painting depicting the skeleton of the Statue of Liberty, a stark contrast to the symbolism embodied by the "Goddess of Democracy" during the events of 1989. This exemplifies the evolving perspectives of Chinese nationalists during this period.

However, amid the apparent resentment toward Western notions of liberty during this era, it is crucial to acknowledge that the desire for Western democracy persisted among Chinese nationalists. What they resisted were not the ideals of Western democracy itself, but rather the Western model of democratization and the accompanying theories of development. Chinese nationalists believed that the process of westernization had contributed to China's national and cultural identity crises. Consequently, they advocated for a separation between China's modernization and westernization, emphasizing the need for a process of "Chinesenization" instead (Zheng, 1999, p. 53).

According to these nationalists, China's future development should be based on an approach that preserves and cultivates its unique Chinese identity and values. They viewed the uncritical adoption of Western models as a threat to China's cultural integrity. Their concerns stemmed from the belief that an excessive embrace of Western ideals could erode China's distinctiveness and hinder the nation's ability to assert its own path to development. By promoting the concept of "Chinesenization," Chinese nationalists sought to foster a modernization process that retained and revitalized China's rich cultural heritage. They aimed to reconcile the pursuit of economic progress and political reform with the preservation of Chinese traditions, customs, and social cohesion. This perspective reflected a nuanced and complex relationship with the West, acknowledging the potential benefits of modernization while asserting the importance of maintaining China's own identity and guiding its development accordingly.

In summary, Chinese nationalists in this era simultaneously expressed resentment toward Western liberties while maintaining a desire for Western-style democracy. Their resistance was primarily directed at the Western model of democratization and theories of development, which they believed were causing identity crises within China. The nationalists advocated for a process of "Chinesenization" that would safeguard China's cultural integrity and shape its future development in alignment with its unique identity and values.

Phase 4

However, the anti-westernization narrative began to undergo a transformation after 2001, coinciding with the rise of China's post-1980s generation and the remarkable achievements China made during that period. In 2001, Beijing was elected as the host city for the 2008 Olympic Games, Shanghai successfully hosted the Asia-Pacific Economic Cooperation summit, China became a member of the WTO, and the national football team qualified for the World Cup for the first time in China's history. This pivotal year was often referred to as the "Chinese year" and was seen as a significant milestone for China in the new century, signifying its growing prominence and achievements (China Economy Website 2009).

These accomplishments served as catalysts for a shift in the nationalist narrative, replacing the discourse of China's "national and cultural identity crises" attributed to westernization with a new wave of pride and a "victor narrative." The emerging post-1980s generation, inspired by these achievements and a sense of national pride, began to embrace a more positive outlook on China's place in the world. The remarkable events of 2001, along with subsequent developments, instilled a sense of confidence and optimism among the Chinese population. The successes in hosting international events, joining influential global organizations, and achieving sporting milestones bolstered national pride and fostered a collective belief in China's capabilities and potential. This shift in narrative reflected a growing confidence in China's ability to navigate its own path of development while engaging with the international community. Rather than perceiving westernization as a threat to China's cultural and national identity, the focus shifted toward showcasing China's achievements and aspirations on the global stage. It is important to note that this narrative shift does not imply a complete abandonment of nationalist sentiments or a wholesale adoption of Western values. Rather, it represents a nuanced evolution in the understanding of China's place in the world and a recognition of its capacity to shape its own future while simultaneously engaging with the global community.

In summary, the narrative surrounding anti-westernization in China began to change after 2001, fueled by the rise of the post-1980s generation and the significant achievements that marked that period. China's successes in hosting international events, joining global organizations, and achieving notable milestones shifted the nationalist narrative from one of identity crises to one of pride and a "victor narrative." This transformation reflected growing confidence in China's capabilities and a desire to assert its own developmental path on the global stage.

Phase 5

The resurgence of Chinese nationalism after 2001, particularly among the younger generation, garnered significant global attention and showcased a powerful and distinct form of nationalism. What set this new wave of nationalists apart was their overwhelming and extreme pride in their country and its central government. Notably, this generation exhibited a unique characteristic whereby the Western "cultural and spiritual fast food" that had been questioned by the previous generation of nationalists was now embraced and beloved. This shift in attitude reflects a paradoxical relationship with the West among the young nationalists. On one hand, there is a fervent embrace of Western culture, highlighting the appeal of Western music, fashion, entertainment, and lifestyle. Western influences have permeated various aspects of their lives, shaping their preferences and aspirations. However, alongside this embrace of Western culture, there is a sharp resentment toward Western political ideologies. The young nationalists maintain a distinct aversion to Western political systems and the perceived interference of Western countries in China's affairs. This paradoxical stance reflects a complex and nuanced perspective on the West, combining a fascination with its cultural products while maintaining a guarded attitude toward its political values.

This new wave of nationalists represents a departure from the previous anti/pro-Western dichotomy. Their evolving ideology demonstrates a more multifaceted and nuanced understanding of the West. While they embrace and consume Western cultural products, they remain wary of Western political ideologies that they perceive as potential threats to China's stability and sovereignty. It is important to recognize that this paradoxical relationship with the West does not represent a unified stance among all young nationalists, as views can vary. However, the overall trend indicates a shift in nationalist sentiment from a purely anti-Western stance to a more complex and contradictory set of attitudes. This resurgence of Chinese nationalism after 2001, particularly among the younger generation, showcased a powerful and distinct form of nationalism characterized by extreme pride in the country and its central government. This new wave of nationalists exhibits a paradoxical relationship with the West, simultaneously embracing Western culture while harboring resentment toward Western political ideologies. This shift in ideology represents a more nuanced and multifaceted understanding of the West among young nationalists in China.

The emergence of the internet as a platform for expression has become a defining characteristic of this new wave of nationalist sentiment, particularly among the younger generation who are the first to grow up with widespread internet access in China. The internet has played a significant role in shaping and amplifying their nationalistic sentiments. In the online realm, consumerism and consumerist ideologies tend to dominate, as evidenced by the prevalence of online shopping, entertainment, and social media consumption among the young generation. However, alongside this consumerist focus, there is also a notable passion for political issues related to China's image and national interests, which is disseminated and strengthened through online platforms.

The internet provides a space for young nationalists in China to express their views, engage in discussions, and mobilize support for various causes related to China's national image. It serves as a powerful tool for spreading and disseminating information, enabling the amplification of nationalist sentiments and the mobilization of like-minded individuals. Online platforms, including social media, discussion forums, and video-sharing sites, allow young nationalists to connect with one another, share their perspectives, and rally around common causes. These platforms facilitate the rapid dissemination of ideas, images, and narratives that support their nationalist beliefs. It is important to note that the online landscape is diverse, and not all online spaces are solely dedicated to nationalist sentiments. However, the internet has undeniably played a significant role in shaping and amplifying the nationalist discourse among the younger generation in China. It has provided them with a powerful tool for expression and mobilization, allowing their nationalistic sentiments to spread and gain traction.

In summary, the internet has become a distinct feature of this new wave of nationalism among the younger generation in China. It serves as a platform for the expression and mobilization of their nationalistic sentiments, alongside the prevailing consumerist ideologies. While consumerism dominates online behaviors, the passion for political issues concerning China's image is also spread and strengthened through the internet. The online realm provides young nationalists with a space to connect, share ideas, and engage in discussions related to China's national interests, shaping their perspectives and enabling the dissemination of nationalist narratives.

Phase 6

The year 2016 marked a significant turning point in China's nationalism, triggered by two key factors that had a profound impact on the national sentiment. The first trigger was the release of "Made in China 2025," a 10-year plan aimed at modernizing China's manufacturing base through the rapid development of 10 high-tech industries. This plan showcased China's ambitions to become a global leader in advanced technology and innovation, instilling a sense of national pride and confidence in China's capabilities. The second trigger was the release of the Chinese war action film, *Wolf Warrior*. Directed and starring Chinese action film star Wu Jing, with Scott Adkins in a prominent role, *Wolf Warrior* was released on April 2, 2015, after a seven-year hiatus. The film quickly gained attention and garnered significant commercial success, grossing $51 million. However, it was the sequel, *Wolf Warrior II*, released on July 27, 2017, that became a game-changer in China's film industry history. It shattered box office records and emerged as the highest-grossing Chinese film ever released. What made *Wolf Warrior II* distinct was its unique combination of action-packed sequences and the inclusion of the People's Liberation Army special forces, which strengthened the collective sense of pride and confidence in China as a nation.

The film's tagline, "Anyone who offends China will be killed no matter how far the target is," quickly went viral on Chinese social media platform Weibo. This bold and assertive message resonated deeply with Chinese audiences, reflecting a desire to showcase China's strength and determination on the global stage. Liu (2017, p. 258) describes this phenomenon, stating,

"China is anxious to flex its muscles in front of domestic and international audiences after hundreds of years of shame. Driven by the slogan of 'anyone who offends China will be destroyed no matter where it is,' the film appeals to the most simplified and rough national imagination." The combination of "Made in China 2025" and the success of the *Wolf Warrior* films sparked a renewed sense of national pride and confidence among the Chinese population. These triggers tapped into a deep-seated desire to shed the historical narrative of China's perceived weakness and to assert its position as a powerful and influential nation on the global stage.

The year 2016 marked a significant shift in Chinese nationalism due to the release of "Made in China 2025" and the success of the *Wolf Warrior* films. These triggers ignited a sense of national pride and confidence by showcasing China's technological advancements and military capabilities. The films, in particular, captured the imagination of Chinese audiences and resonated with their desire for a strong and assertive China.

The impact of *Wolf Warrior II* went beyond its commercial success and resonated on a global scale. In China, the film created a sensation, breaking numerous box office records and earning a staggering 1.6 billion yuan in just one week (BBC, 2020). This remarkable response not only solidified its position as a domestic hit but also propelled it to the top of the global box office, surpassing Hollywood blockbuster *Dunkirk* (BBC, 2020). Film critics recognized the significance of *Wolf Warrior II* beyond its entertainment value. They acknowledged that the film represented a mature commercial genre that had broader implications for the development of main theme movies in China, making them more robust and aiding their entry into the global market (Zeng, 2017). The success of *Wolf Warrior II* demonstrated China's potential to produce commercially successful films that could captivate both domestic and international audiences.

The timing of the film's premiere also played a role in its success. It coincided with the 90th anniversary of the founding of the Chinese army, which further heightened the patriotic fervor surrounding the movie. The release of the film just ahead of this significant anniversary created a sense of national pride and unity among Chinese audiences, contributing to its massive popularity and cultural impact. The image of Wu Jing, the actor who played the main role in *Wolf Warrior II*, became a symbol of national pride and resilience. His portrayal of a strong and heroic character resonated deeply with Chinese audiences and went beyond the realm of the film. During the Tokyo Olympics, Wu Jing's image was frequently used as a representation of national pride and as a means to express disappointment or frustration toward other nations, showcasing the film's enduring influence on the Chinese consciousness. *Wolf Warrior II* not only achieved extraordinary commercial success in China but also made a significant impact globally. The film's record-breaking box office performance, its implications for the development of Chinese cinema, and its timing in conjunction with a significant anniversary all contributed to its success. The movie's main theme of national pride, embodied by the lead actor Wu Jing, further solidified its cultural impact, as his image became synonymous with Chinese resilience and patriotism.

Since 2016, there has been a noticeable shift in Chinese sentiment toward the West, characterized by a growing assertiveness and national pride, particularly in China's handling of the COVID-19 pandemic. This shift has had implications for the younger generation, who are exhibiting changing attitudes toward the West, and one notable aspect of this change is their diminishing desire to consume foreign brands. China's expression of ambition and assertiveness in recent years has contributed to a renewed sense of national pride among its young generation. The country's achievements in various domains, including technology, innovation, and its effective response to the COVID-19 pandemic, have bolstered confidence in China's capabilities and fostered a sense of unity and pride among its citizens.

This changing sentiment toward the West is reflected in the decreasing desire to consume foreign brands. In the past, Western brands held a strong allure for Chinese consumers, symbolizing prestige, quality, and modernity. However, as Chinese nationalism and confidence in domestic products have grown, there has been a shift toward favoring homegrown brands. This trend can be attributed to several factors, including a desire to support local industries, an emphasis on national self-sufficiency, and a belief in the quality and innovation of Chinese products. Furthermore, the changing sentiment toward foreign brands also reflects a broader shift in Chinese society. The younger generation, in particular, is becoming more discerning and mindful of the cultural, economic, and geopolitical implications of their consumption choices. There is a growing recognition that supporting domestic brands aligns with a sense of national pride and contributes to the overall development and prosperity of China. This shift does not imply a complete rejection of Western influence or products. Rather, it signals a more nuanced and balanced approach toward consumption. Chinese consumers are increasingly looking for products that not only meet their needs but also align with their values and aspirations as Chinese citizens. This trend has paved the way for the rise of successful domestic brands in various sectors, including technology, fashion, and lifestyle, which are gaining popularity and recognition both within China and internationally.

In summary, the changing sentiments of China's young generation toward the West since 2016 have manifested in a shift away from a strong desire for foreign brands. This shift is driven by growing national pride, confidence in domestic products, and a more discerning approach to consumption. It reflects a desire to support local industries and align consumption choices with broader cultural and national aspirations. While the West still holds influence in certain aspects, the rise of successful domestic brands indicates a changing landscape of consumer preferences in China.

Consequences

Based on a case study of 45 incidents that occurred between 2016 and 2021, the consequences can be summarized as follows:

Political Triggers: Out of the 44 cases examined, 36 of them were attributed to political triggers. These triggers included issues related to Hong Kong, Taiwan, Tibet, the South China Sea, and the deployment of the THAAD missile defense system. These incidents often involved tensions and disputes between China and other countries or regions.

Racism or Defamation: The remaining nine cases were primarily driven by racism or defamation, where negative remarks or actions targeted at Chinese individuals or the Chinese nation were involved.

Consequences: While the majority of the 44 cases had minor consequences, nine cases stood out due to their significant impacts. It is worth noting that all nine cases with significant consequences were linked to political triggers, demonstrating the strong influence of political factors on the outcomes. However, there was one exceptional case that resulted from discrimination, which had the most significant overall consequences.

The significant consequences mentioned under "Racism or Defamation" indicate that these incidents had a profound impact, potentially resulting in substantial losses. In one instance, it was noted that the loss amounted to 98 percent of the Chinese market. This highlights the potential economic repercussions and the sensitivity of Chinese consumers to incidents related to politics or discrimination.

Overall, the case study reveals that political triggers played a dominant role in shaping the incidents analyzed, with consequences ranging from minor to significant. While the majority of cases resulted from political tensions, it is crucial to recognize that incidents related to discrimination had the potential to yield the most far-reaching and severe outcomes. This highlights the importance of understanding the broader context and sensitivities when

Table 3.2 Cases with significant consequences.

Brand Name	Trigger and Year	Consequences
Lotte Mart	helped THAAD deployment in the Republic of Korea (2017)	significant, withdrew from the Chinese market in 2018, and all 99 shops were closed
APA Hotel	right-wing books denying Nanjing Massacre (2017)	significant, banned by National Tourism Administration
D&G	discrimination (2018)	significant, lost 98% market
NBA	Hong Kong (2019)	significant, still banned by CCTV
Nike	Xinjiang (2021)	significant, sales on Tmall dropped by 59% in April
H&M	Xinjiang (2021)	significant, sales in China dropped by 45% in half year
Uniqlo	Xinjiang (2021)	significant, sales in April on Tmall dropped by 20%
Muji	Xinjiang (2021)	significant, its share price fell by 7% on April 15th, claimed to continue to use cotton from Xinjiang
Adidas	Xinjiang (2021)	significant, sales in the Asian-Pacific area drop by 15.9% in the second-quarter of 2021, sales in April on Tmall dropped by 78%

Source: Author's own compilation.

engaging with China and its people, as well as the potential risks involved in missteps related to politics or discrimination.

(See Table 3.2 of nine cases with significant consequences below; for full list of 44 cases see Appendix.)

Conclusion

This chapter delves into the historical context of Chinese consumer nationalism, exploring the characteristics of each wave and shedding light on how it has evolved in recent years. It aims to provide readers with a comprehensive understanding of the changes that have taken place, the role of the government and state media in each wave, and the potential consequences that may arise from the emergence of new waves. By exploring this intricate interplay between different actors and forces, the chapter aims to provide readers with a nuanced understanding of Chinese consumer nationalism. It recognizes the multifaceted nature of this phenomenon and emphasizes the need to consider both top-down and bottom-up influences in order to grasp its complexities fully.

It is crucial to avoid oversimplifying the dynamics behind Chinese consumer nationalism by attributing its actions solely to either the government or grassroots movements. In reality, the landscape is much more complex. There are instances where consumer nationalism is initiated through social media channels, gaining traction and subsequently receiving endorsement from state-controlled media outlets like China Central Television (CCTV). However, it is important to note that even in such cases, CCTV has been known to call for "rationality" in response to antiforeign sentiments. This is because there is a recognition that such movements, if left unchecked, can lead to unintended consequences such as open criticism toward the Chinese government itself.

In essence, the phenomenon of Chinese consumer nationalism involves a combination of both "top-down" and "bottom-up" influences. State media closely monitors the sentiments and actions of consumers, stepping in when necessary to guide or shape the narrative. This dynamic reflects a symbiotic relationship between the government, state media, and the broader consumer base, where actions and reactions are intricately intertwined.

Chapter 4

TYPOLOGY STUDY OF CHINESE CONSUMER NATIONALISM

This chapter delves into a crucial aspect of the existing research on nationalism in China, highlighting a notable issue that has emerged. The prevailing approach has tended to examine Chinese nationalistic sentiments as a unified whole, neglecting the inherent complexity and diversity within this phenomenon. Taking such a holistic perspective is overly simplistic and fails to account for the multifaceted nature of Chinese nationalists' motivations and actions.

To rectify this oversight, it is imperative to categorize the various manifestations of consumer nationalism in China based on a range of indices. By doing so, we can gain a more nuanced understanding of this complex phenomenon. Therefore, this chapter aims to explore the distinct types of consumer nationalistic actions observed in China and elucidate the varying consequences associated with each type. In order to substantiate this argument, the chapter will present several illustrative cases.

The central contention put forth in this chapter is that contemporary consumer nationalism in China can be effectively classified into three distinct types, each engendering a different level of consequences. By differentiating these types, we can discern the specific motivations, behaviors, and outcomes associated with each category. This nuanced approach not only enriches our comprehension of consumer nationalism in China but also contributes to a more comprehensive analysis of nationalism studies in general.

Mapping the Field

Nationalism, as a widely acknowledged sentiment shaping both public and private spheres, has been prevalent since the late eighteenth century. Its influence on global politics can be understood through the concept of identifying the state or nation with its people. However, to grasp the concept of "consumer nationalism," it is essential to differentiate it from related terms such as economic nationalism, commercial nationalism, consumer ethnocentrism, political consumerism, and consumer nationalism.

Economic nationalism

The term "economic nationalism" has a historical origin that can be traced back to the early twentieth century. It gained recognition through the works of notable economists and scholars who examined the concept in depth. One of the earliest instances of using this term can be attributed to American economist Alvin Johnson in 1917, who is renowned as one of the cofounders of the New School for Social Research. Alvin Johnson's article marked a significant milestone in the study of economic nationalism, laying the foundation for subsequent academic explorations of the subject. Building upon Johnson's initial work, other scholars and economists delved into various aspects of economic nationalism, further expanding its understanding. Among the academics who contributed to this trajectory, Gregory (1931) made notable contributions to the field. His work added insights and perspectives on the economic implications and ramifications of nationalist policies and ideologies. Rappard (1937) also played a significant role in advancing the understanding of economic nationalism. His research delved into the relationship between economic nationalism and international trade, shedding light on the tensions and conflicts that can arise in the context of global economic interactions. Heilperin (1960) made valuable contributions to the field with his studies on the impact of economic nationalism on international monetary systems. His work explored how nationalist economic policies can influence currency exchange rates, capital flows, and the stability of the global financial order. Johnson (1967) continued to contribute to the field of economic nationalism, likely building upon his earlier work. His research likely offered further insights into the various dimensions of economic nationalism, such as its implications for economic development, trade relations, and national identity. Hieronymi (1980) further enriched the understanding of economic nationalism by examining its political and social dimensions. His work likely shed light on how economic nationalism interacts with political ideologies and social structures, shaping the broader dynamics of nations and societies.

The term "economic nationalism" finds frequent usage in the field of political science, particularly within the context of international relations. Scholars and researchers in this discipline have extensively examined economic nationalism as an aspect of broader nationalist ideologies. Several notable works have contributed to the understanding of economic nationalism in this field. Gilpin (1984), Crane (1998), Abdelal (2001), Helleiner (2002), Pickel and

Jacqui (2002), and Nakano (2004) are among the scholars who have explored economic nationalism in the realm of international relations. Their studies have shed light on the interactions between economic policies, nationalism, and global politics. The definitions assigned to economic nationalism can vary across different disciplines. In the realm of economics, scholars have often associated economic nationalism with specific policies. Some of these policies focus on limiting international integration and foreign influence, as discussed by Rappard (1937) and Heilperin (1960). Others are designed to support domestic firms in their competition against foreign counterparts, not only through trade policies but also via subsidies, restrictions on foreign investments aimed at accelerating industrial catch-up or impeding competing nations from catching up, and measures facilitating or fostering cartels. This perspective has been explored by Gregory (1931), Johnson (1967), Kahan (1967), and Hieronymi (1980). The research by these scholars has contributed to a comprehensive understanding of economic nationalism, elucidating its various dimensions and implications. By examining the policies and strategies employed by nations to protect domestic industries, promote national economic interests, and assert control over their economic destiny, these studies have shed light on the complex interplay between economic nationalism, international trade, and global power dynamics.

During the late 1990s and early 2000s, political scientists critically examined and challenged the existing definition of economic nationalism. They argued that the definition lacked rigor and historical context, enabling economists with liberal leanings to label any policy they disagreed with as nationalist (Crane, 1998; Pickel, 2003). These scholars proposed an alternative perspective, emphasizing that economic nationalism should be defined based on motives or what Helleiner (2005) referred to as "nationalist content." They asserted that policies should not be considered economic nationalism unless they are motivated by nationalist thought. According to this viewpoint, the traditional policy prescriptions associated with economic nationalism, as identified by economists, may not necessarily exist. This is because even liberal economic policies can be driven by nationalist thought in certain circumstances (Bolle and Zettelmeyer, 2019). However, scholars acknowledge the difficulty in defining motives since they can vary in different settings. For instance, the preference for public enterprise over private enterprise, observed by Harry Johnson (1965) in the post-colonial states, can be considered part of economic nationalism, even if it is not necessarily motivated by nationalism. Given the complex range of motives, economic nationalism is defined as "policies designed to further domestic economic interests (the interests of domestic producers, consumers, and/or workers) at the expense of foreign economic interests, at least in the short run" (Bolle and Zettelmeyer, 2019,

p. 7). This definition explicitly excludes liberal policies, and the inclusion of "at least in the short run" allows for certain policies, such as infant industry tariffs advocated by Hamilton and List, which aim to level the playing field during a catch-up phase rather than establishing a permanent advantage for domestic interests (ibid.).

While the previously mentioned definition of economic nationalism appears to address the issue of motives, it is important to acknowledge that the definition can vary depending on the specific context in which it is applied. However, certain characteristics can be summarized to provide a general understanding of economic nationalism. At its core, economic nationalism involves favoritism or discrimination in support of one's own nation, implemented as a deliberate policy (Macesich, 1985). Economic nationalism has become associated with a wide range of practices that aim to protect domestic industries and prioritize national economic interests. These practices include protectionism in the form of tariffs, which are taxes imposed on imported goods, as well as quotas that restrict the quantity of foreign products allowed into a domestic market. Additionally, voluntary restraint agreements and countervailing duties, which are tariffs imposed to counterbalance unfair foreign subsidies, are also considered manifestations of economic nationalism (Reich, 1991). Regulatory standards can be another tool employed in economic nationalism, establishing requirements or restrictions that effectively bar foreign products from accessing the domestic market. This can involve imposing technical or safety standards that foreign products may find difficult to meet, creating a barrier to entry (Reich, 1991). Economic nationalism is further observed in practices such as "dumping," which refers to exporting products at prices below the domestic prices of the receiving market. This strategy can undermine local producers and distort fair competition. Governments may also provide subsidies to domestic firms to support their competitiveness or even force the transfer of property from foreign owners to national entities, aiming to enhance domestic control over strategic industries (Johnson, 1967). Economic nationalism can also manifest in the form of counter-trade restrictions, which require reciprocal trade arrangements or impose conditions on foreign companies as a condition for market access (Johnson, 1967). These practices collectively reflect the various dimensions of economic nationalism and highlight the range of measures employed to promote domestic industries, protect national interests, and maintain control over the economy. While the specific policies and practices associated with economic nationalism may differ across countries and contexts, the common thread lies in the deliberate favoritism toward one's own nation in economic matters.

Commercial nationalism

Commercial nationalism refers to the phenomenon where nationalism is intertwined with commercial activities. Yang (2016) provides a concise summary, stating that commercial nationalism represents the convergence of the commercialized production of nationalism and the commercialization of the resulting national identities. This term holds particular relevance in post-socialist contexts like China, where the reduction of state subsidies for national broadcasting coincides with the reshaping of consumer citizenship in nationalistic terms. Additionally, the state itself transforms into an enterprise and assumes the role of a promoter of nationalism (Yang, 2016). In various countries, the state plays a significant role in constructing a national identity, often adopting characteristics associated with commercial branding. Meanwhile, the media industries, driven increasingly by profit motives, become instrumental in shaping discussions on national identity and disseminating branded forms of nationalism and nationalist identities (Volcic and Andrejevic, 2011). This dynamic reflects the influence of market forces on the construction and dissemination of nationalistic narratives. The intertwining of commercial activities and nationalism in commercial nationalism is particularly evident in the ways countries engage in nation-building exercises. The state, acting as an entrepreneur, seeks to create a cohesive national identity that resonates with its citizens, often using marketing techniques to shape public perceptions. By employing branding strategies, the state aims to evoke emotional connections, loyalty, and pride in the nation.

This approach borrows from commercial practices that prioritize image-building, reputation management, and the creation of a distinct national "brand" (Volcic and Andrejevic, 2011). Furthermore, the media plays a crucial role in commercial nationalism, as it becomes a platform for framing issues related to national identity. Media industries, driven by market demands, may present nationalistic narratives in a way that resonates with the target audience and aligns with commercial interests. This can lead to the proliferation of branded forms of nationalism, where national identity is packaged and promoted as a marketable product (Volcic and Andrejevic, 2011). Commercial nationalism represents the fusion of nationalism with commercial activities. It is particularly evident in post-socialist contexts like China, where state subsidies for national broadcasting have declined, and consumer citizenship is reoriented in nationalistic terms. The state, acting as an enterprise, has adopted commercial branding techniques to construct and promote a national identity. Meanwhile, media industries play a pivotal role in framing issues of national identity and disseminating branded forms of nationalism that align with market-driven interests.

The concept of nationalism has been deeply intertwined with the history of capitalism since its inception. Therefore, it is not surprising that changes in the economy associated with neoliberalization and globalization have coincided with corresponding developments in nationalism (Volcic and Andrejevic, 2011). Commercial nationalism serves as a link between political and commercial actors, particularly through the practice of nation branding. The term "nation branding" was coined by British brand consultant Simon Anholt in the late 1990s. It is built on the assumption that the global popularity of consumer products is closely connected to the international reputation of the nations producing them (Castello and Mihelj, 2018). An influential early work on nation branding by Anholt (1998) highlighted that many successful international brands originate from countries that themselves possess a strong brand image. It emphasized the transfer of imagery and brand equity that often occurs between successful consumer brands and the nations they represent (Anholt, 1998, p. 395). Following this period, a significant body of work emerged with the objective of providing guidance to states and other actors interested in harnessing the power of nationalism to bolster their economies and enhance their international image. Researchers and practitioners sought to understand how nations could strategically shape their brand identities to attract investment, tourism, and consumer loyalty. Notable works in this field include Anholt (2006), Dinnie (2008), and Olins (1999).

These works delved into various aspects of nation branding, exploring techniques for effectively positioning and promoting national brands in the global marketplace. They examined strategies to enhance a nation's reputation, create positive associations with its products and culture, and ultimately generate economic benefits through increased consumer interest and engagement. By focusing on nation branding, commercial nationalism establishes a connection between political actors, who shape national policies and identities, and commercial actors, who leverage these identities to strengthen their brands. It reflects the recognition that the economic success and global competitiveness of a nation are intertwined with its reputation, image, and ability to resonate with consumers on a global scale. The integration of nationalism and capitalism has paved the way for the emergence of commercial nationalism. Within this framework, nation branding has gained prominence as a means to leverage nationalism for economic and reputational gains. Scholars and practitioners have developed guidance and strategies to assist states and other actors in effectively harnessing the power of nationalism to bolster their economies and enhance their international standing.

Since its inception, nation branding has experienced rapid evolution, becoming a complex process that brings together a diverse array of political and commercial actors (Castello and Mihelj, 2018). This evolution has given rise to a dual process, as highlighted by Kania-Lundholm (2014), wherein the commercial becomes nationalized, and the national becomes commercialized. This dual process captures the simultaneous utilization of nationalism by commercial entities to promote their goods and services, as well as the adoption of marketing techniques by states to cultivate successful nation brands. On one hand, commercial entities recognize the potential of nationalism as a tool to enhance their market appeal. By leveraging nationalistic sentiments, businesses seek to establish stronger connections with consumers and instill a sense of loyalty and pride in their products or services. This can involve incorporating national symbols, narratives, or cultural references into branding and marketing strategies, aligning their offerings with notions of national identity and heritage. On the other hand, states have embraced marketing tactics to develop and promote successful nation brands. Drawing from the principles of commercial branding, states employ strategies to shape their national image, attract investments, boost tourism, and foster a positive perception of their country on the global stage. They utilize branding techniques to position their nation as unique, desirable, and competitive, emphasizing cultural assets, natural beauty, historical significance, or economic strengths. This process often involves collaboration between government bodies, tourism boards, cultural institutions, and other stakeholders to craft a compelling national narrative. The concept of "commercial nationalism," as proposed by Volčič and Andrejevic (2015), encapsulates this broad range of phenomena that emerge when states and societies view themselves as entities akin to corporations, seeking to derive economic benefits from their national culture. It reflects the convergence of nationalist ideologies and market-oriented approaches, where the nation is perceived as a valuable asset that can be monetized and leveraged for economic gain.

The concept of commercial nationalism finds particular relevance in the context of mainland China, where commercial media outlets have been observed to promote a more aggressive form of nationalism compared to state-run media (Seo, 2008). This trend has been accompanied by swift actions taken by companies in response to any potential damage to the national image, with frequent public announcements on Weibo regarding the disassociation of brands from certain individuals. As early as more than a decade ago, it was noted that China's fast-growing cultural industry was actively involved in manufacturing and disseminating nationalistic discourses (Soe, 2008, p. 1). Examining another nation, Ju (2007) argues that the phenomenon known as the "Korean wave"—the widespread popularity of Korean popular culture in other parts of Asia—exemplifies the fusion of commercial culture and nationalism. This serves as evidence that the logic of globalization does not necessarily oppose the propagation of nationalism. Ju suggests that contemporary forms of local identity can be seen as products of the global context, where particular brand identities are carved out in response to the ongoing process of globalization (Ju, 2007, p. 9). In line with the insights of Seo (2007; 2008), Ju (2007), and other scholars (Turner, 2010; Volcic, 2009; White, 2009), Volcic and Andrejevic (2011, p. 613) summarize the concept of commercial nationalism as the intentional utilization of nationalist appeals by commercial entities to differentiate their products within a competitive and increasingly interconnected global marketplace.

This notion recognizes that commercial entities strategically employ nationalism as a means to set themselves apart from their competitors. By aligning their products or services with patriotic sentiments and national identity, they seek to attract consumers who are drawn to the notion of supporting their country's economy or culture. This deliberate fusion of commercial appeals and nationalism acknowledges the power of collective identification and emotional attachments to a nation as influential factors in consumer decision-making. The phenomenon of commercial nationalism highlights the intricate relationship between market dynamics and nationalist sentiments. It demonstrates how commercial entities navigate the global marketplace by incorporating nationalist themes into their branding strategies, capitalizing on consumers' emotional connections to their nation and leveraging the values associated with national identity to promote their products or services. In summary, commercial nationalism manifests in various contexts, including mainland China's media landscape and the popularity of Korean popular culture across Asia. It signifies the intentional use of nationalist appeals by commercial entities to differentiate themselves in a competitive global market. This phenomenon underscores the significant role played by national identity and patriotism in shaping consumer behavior and illustrates the complex interplay between commerce and nationalism in the contemporary era of globalization.

Consumer ethnocentrism

Consumer ethnocentrism stems from the broader concept of ethnocentrism, which was first introduced by William Graham Sumner over a century ago in 1906. Ethnocentrism can be understood as the inherent tendency of individuals to perceive their own social or cultural group as superior, regarding it as the center of the universe. This perspective leads people to interpret and evaluate other social units based on the standards and values of their own group, often resulting in the rejection of individuals who exhibit cultural dissimilarities while embracing those who share similar cultural characteristics (Shimp and Sharma, 1987, p. 280). Consumer ethnocentrism specifically relates to the domain of consumer behavior, encompassing the beliefs and attitudes of individuals regarding the purchase and consumption of goods and services. It reflects the inclination of consumers to favor products or brands originating from their own country or cultural group over those from foreign sources. Consumer ethnocentrism is characterized by a preference for domestic products and a bias against foreign products, driven by the belief that local offerings are superior in terms of quality, reliability, or value. This phenomenon arises from the psychological need for individuals to maintain a sense of identity and group affiliation. By supporting domestic products, consumers express their loyalty and support for their own culture, economy, and national interests. Consumer ethnocentrism can manifest in various ways, such as the willingness to pay higher prices for domestic products, a preference for locally produced goods, or a reluctance to purchase foreign brands. Consumer ethnocentrism is influenced by various factors, including cultural, social, and economic considerations. Cultural values, national pride, historical experiences, and perceptions of national superiority or uniqueness can significantly shape consumers' ethnocentric attitudes. Social influences, such as family, peers, and media, can also contribute to the formation and reinforcement of consumer ethnocentrism. It is important to note that while consumer ethnocentrism may impact consumers' purchasing decisions, it does not necessarily imply a complete rejection of foreign products. Consumers may exhibit varying degrees of ethnocentrism, and factors such as product quality, price, availability, and personal preferences can still influence their choices. Furthermore, globalization and cultural exchange have led to the emergence of cosmopolitan consumers who actively seek and embrace diversity in their consumption patterns, challenging the boundaries of consumer ethnocentrism. Consumer ethnocentrism is rooted in the broader concept of ethnocentrism, representing individuals' inclination to favor domestic products and exhibit a bias against foreign alternatives. It arises from the psychological need for identity and group affiliation, reflecting loyalty and support for one's own culture and nation. Cultural, social, and economic factors shape consumer ethnocentrism, but its impact on actual consumer behavior can vary. The dynamic nature of consumer ethnocentrism underscores the ongoing complexities of consumer decision-making in an interconnected global marketplace.

The concept of ethnocentrism was introduced to the field of marketing as a potential factor capable of influencing and shaping consumer behavior (Javalgi et al., 2005). Subsequently, it has been recognized as a human inclination capable of influencing consumer choices across various purchasing scenarios (Boieji et al., 2010). Shimp and Sharma (1987), pioneering scholars in consumer studies, were the first to incorporate the concept of ethnocentrism into the examination of marketing and consumer behavior. They coined the term "consumer ethnocentric tendencies" (CET) (Sharma, Shimp, and Shin, 1995). Consumer ethnocentrism refers to the beliefs held by consumers regarding the appropriateness and morality of purchasing products made in foreign countries (Shimp and Sharma, 1987, p. 280). It is widely accepted that consumer ethnocentrism has a negative impact on consumers' intention to purchase foreign products. This means that individuals with high ethnocentric tendencies tend to hold unfavorable attitudes toward buying imported products. Shimp and Sharma (1987) assert that consumers refuse to purchase foreign products due to concerns about their detrimental effects on the national economy and the potential for unemployment. Likewise, Wetzels, De Ruyter, and Van Birgelen (1998) highlight the influence of patriotic sentiments, which lead consumers to reject foreign-made products. Consequently, consumers who strongly embrace ethnocentrism are generally uninterested in consuming foreign goods and services, primarily due to the shared belief that such behavior is morally wrong and has detrimental consequences for the local economy (Strizhakova, Coulter, and Price, 2008). The degree of ethnocentrism can vary among individual consumers (Shimp, 1984; Durvasula, Andrews, and Netemeyer, 1997; Vida and Fairhurst, 1999), across different regions within a single country (Shimp and Sharma, 1987), and even between countries as a whole (Becic, 2017; Huddleston, Good, and Stoel 2001; Lantz and Loeb, 1996).

CET is a factor that can influence consumers' choices between domestic and foreign products. Specifically, it directly impacts consumers' inclination to purchase foreign products (Silili and Karunaratna, 2014). Consumer ethnocentrism refers to the tendency of buyers to avoid imported products based on nationalistic reasons, regardless of price or quality considerations (Shankarmahesh, 2006, p. 147). Studies consistently demonstrate a cause-effect relationship between consumer ethnocentrism and negative attitudes toward foreign products (Sharma, Shimp, and Shin, 1995). As a result, ethnocentrism holds significant importance in international marketing as it can pose challenges for companies seeking to enter overseas markets (Altintas and Tokol, 2007, p. 309). Okechuku (1994) and Good and Huddleston (1995) argue that consumer ethnocentrism is prevalent in highly industrialized countries. Research conducted in developed nations consistently reveals that ethnocentric consumers prefer domestic products over foreign ones (Shimp and Sharma, 1987; Granzin and Painter, 2001; Suh and Kwon, 2002; Marín, 2005; Balabanis and Diamantopoulos, 2004). However, there is some ambiguity regarding this relationship in certain developing countries (Agbonifoh and Elimimian, 1999; Bahaee and Pisani, 2009; Hamin and Elliott, 2006; Samoui, 2009; Wang and Chen, 2004).

The notion of "consumer ethnocentrism" and its corresponding measurement tool, the CETSCALE, introduced by Shimp and Sharma (1987), has gained significant traction in the field. Initially, consumer ethnocentrism was defined as consumers' beliefs concerning the "suitability and moral implications" of buying products made in foreign countries. Ethnocentric consumers hold the view that purchasing imported products should be avoided as it negatively impacts the domestic economy, leads to job losses, and is deemed unpatriotic (Shimp and Sharma, 1987, p. 280).

Consumer nationalism

Consumer nationalism, as a phenomenon, has gained prominence in recent years. It reflects the growing sentiment among consumers to assert their national identity and exhibit loyalty toward products and brands originating from their own country. This form of nationalism is not necessarily driven by explicit government policies but is rather fueled by consumer-led movements and grassroots initiatives. One of the ways consumer nationalism manifests is through campaigns and initiatives that encourage the purchase of domestic products. These "Buy Domestic" movements, often characterized by slogans and appeals to national pride, aim to promote local industries and support the domestic economy. By choosing locally produced goods and services, consumers believe they are contributing to job creation, economic growth, and the overall well-being of their nation. Wang (2006) defines consumer nationalism as the deliberate invocation of collective national identities during the process of consumption. This can manifest in various ways, including favoring products and brands from one's own country and expressing reluctance or rejection toward those from foreign countries. The concept of consumer nationalism extends beyond tangible products to include media and entertainment offerings, where preferences for domestic content and cultural representation play a significant role. In the context of international tourism, consumer nationalism influences destination choices. Travelers may prioritize visiting locations that align with their national identity or cultural heritage. They seek authentic experiences that resonate with their sense of patriotism, leading to a preference for destinations that showcase their own country's unique attributes. Consumer nationalism reflects a complex interplay between economic, cultural, and emotional factors. It taps into the pride individuals feel for their nation and their desire to support and promote local industries. As globalization continues to shape the world, consumer nationalism serves as a counterforce, asserting the importance of national identity and fostering a sense of belonging and solidarity among consumers within a given country.

Existing research on consumer nationalism often places greater emphasis on consumer practices and behaviors rather than consumer beliefs. Specifically, studies tend to focus on instances of militant and politicized consumer nationalism, where consumption is utilized as a tool to exert economic and political pressure on other nations. These studies examine the intentional use of consumption to inflict damage or send a strong message to a specific country or its products. For instance, Ashenfelter, Ciccarella, and Howard (2007), Cuadras and Raya (2016), Fershtman and Gandal (1998), and Li (2009) delve into the realm of politicized consumer nationalism. They explore how consumers actively engage in boycotts, sanctions, or selective purchasing to express their dissatisfaction with a particular country or to support their own nation in times of political tension or conflict. These studies delve into the motivations, strategies, and economic implications of these actions, shedding light on the linkages between consumption and nationalism in a highly politicized context. By focusing on the practical aspects of consumer nationalism, these studies provide valuable insights into the ways in which consumption can be employed as a tool for economic and political activism. They explore the dynamics of consumer choices, decision-making processes, and collective actions that aim to exert influence or achieve specific outcomes on a national or international scale. It is important to note that while these studies concentrate on the more militant and politicized forms of consumer nationalism, consumer beliefs and attitudes still underlie such behaviors. Consumers who engage in these practices often hold strong nationalistic sentiments, which serve as the driving force behind their consumption-related actions. Therefore, while less attention may be given to consumer beliefs in these studies, they remain a foundational aspect of understanding and contextualizing the behaviors and practices associated with militant consumer nationalism.

The widely used definition of consumer nationalism, as provided by Karl Gerth (2011, p. 280), focuses on the political dimension of consumption. It characterizes consumer nationalism as the deliberate act of making a political statement through the non-consumption of products from a disliked country or countries and actively choosing to consume goods and services produced domestically. However, this definition fails to capture the full breadth of consumer nationalism, as pointed out by Castello. Castello highlights that Gerth's definition represents only one facet of consumer nationalism, overlooking the more subtle and commonplace intersections of consumption and nationalism. These include everyday practices such as wearing T-shirts adorned with national symbols, opting for national dishes in restaurants, or routinely purchasing locally produced goods from a neighborhood supermarket. These acts occur without a specific political agenda but still contribute to the expression of national identity and consumer preferences. By expanding

the understanding of consumer nationalism beyond its overtly political manifestations, researchers can gain insights into the multifaceted ways in which
consumption intertwines with nationalism in daily life. These more diffuse
and mundane expressions of consumer nationalism, although seemingly
unremarkable, play a significant role in shaping individuals' sense of belonging, cultural identification, and the reinforcement of national pride. To comprehensively grasp the complexities of consumer nationalism, it is crucial to
consider both its overtly political dimensions, as outlined by Gerth's definition, and the subtler expressions that encompass the routine and non-polit-
ical choices individuals make in their consumption patterns. This broader
perspective provides a more holistic understanding of how nationalism and
consumption intersect, capturing the full range of ways in which individuals
engage with and express their national identity through their consumption
practices.

Castello and his team offer a distinct perspective on defining consumer
nationalism. They approach consumer nationalism within the framework of
economic nationalism, wherein commercial and consumer nationalism are
considered integral components of economic nationalism. In this view, economic nationalism prioritizes economic practices such as selling, advertising,
and consumption, emphasizing their significance in shaping national identity. Within the context of economic nationalism, consumer nationalism is
regarded as a collection of discourses and practices that attribute national
importance to consumer objects, including goods and services. Castello,
being a prominent researcher in the field of consumer nationalism, highlights
a notable difference between this definition and previous ones. According
to Castello (2017), consumer actions are not isolated but interconnected
with other actors in the process. This perspective recognizes that consumer
nationalism involves various stakeholders such as retailers, advertisers, marketers, and local producers. These actors actively engage in utilizing discur-
sive means to influence consumers and stimulate specific acts of consumption.
Thus, consumer nationalism is seen as a dynamic interplay between individual consumers and commercial entities, where both parties play significant
roles in shaping and reinforcing nationalistic sentiments through consumption-related discourses and practices.

Upon careful examination and comparison of various terms such as
economic nationalism, commercial nationalism, consumer ethnocentrism,
and consumer nationalism, this book has deliberately chosen to focus on
the concept of "consumer nationalism." This selection is primarily driven
by the research's specific emphasis on studying the attitudes and behaviors
of consumers, rather than solely focusing on their beliefs. While economic
nationalism and commercial nationalism pertain more broadly to economic

practices and the involvement of commercial entities in shaping nationalistic sentiments, consumer ethnocentrism specifically relates to consumers' beliefs about the appropriateness of purchasing foreign-made products. However, these terms do not fully capture the comprehensive scope of the research, which delves into the intricate interplay of consumer attitudes and behaviors within the context of nationalism. By opting for the term "consumer nationalism," this book takes into account the dynamic nature of consumers' attitudes and behaviors as they relate to their national identity. The term encompasses a wider range of consumer actions and expressions, including purchasing preferences, consumption practices, and symbolic acts that reflect national pride and affiliation. The focus on attitudes and behaviors within consumer nationalism aligns with the research's aim of understanding how consumers manifest their national identity through their actions in the marketplace. By exploring consumer attitudes and behaviors, the research seeks to shed light on the nuanced and multifaceted ways in which individuals engage with and express their nationalistic inclinations through consumption-related decisions and practices. In summary, the deliberate choice of "consumer nationalism" as the term of focus in this research reflects the intention to examine consumer attitudes and behaviors within the context of national identity, while acknowledging the distinctiveness and relevance of these aspects in understanding the complex relationship between consumers and nationalism.

Typology of Consumer Nationalism in General

Political consumer nationalism and symbolic consumer nationalism

The well-known approach to categorize consumer nationalism is presented by Castello in his highly influential article "Selling and Consuming the Nation: Understanding Consumer Nationalism" where he delves into a comprehensive and systematic examination of the issue, specifically focusing on two groups: political consumer nationalism (PCN) and symbolic consumer nationalism (SCN). Castello defines PCN as a form of political consumerism that revolves around promoting or hindering the consumption of specific national products. The objective is to impact a nation's economy and, consequently, advance or undermine a particular nation's political agenda. To illustrate this concept, Castello draws on Holzer's discussion of political consumerism, where Holzer defines "role mobilization" as the act of collectively aligning one's personal choices during the purchasing process (p. 140). Within the context of PCN, the "role" refers to an individual's national identity, which serves as a conduit for achieving political goals (Holzer, 2006, p. 406). By examining PCN and SCN, Castello offers a nuanced understanding of the multifaceted nature of consumer nationalism. This categorization provides a framework for analyzing the various ways in which individuals engage in consuming and displaying their national identity. Furthermore, it underscores the significance of economic choices in the broader political landscape, demonstrating how consumer behavior can be leveraged to exert political influence. Overall, Castello's research expands our knowledge of consumer nationalism by shedding light on the interplay between political and symbolic dimensions. By delineating the concepts of PCN and SCN, he enhances our comprehension of how individuals mobilize their national identity through consumption practices, thereby impacting the economic and political spheres.

Expanding on Neilson's work (2010), Castello further refines the categorization of PCN by identifying two distinct subtypes within this framework. These subtypes encompass nationalist boycotts and nationalist buycotts, each characterized by different consumer behaviors and objectives. The first subtype of PCN, nationalist boycotts, involves individuals or groups actively abstaining from purchasing products associated with a specific nation. This form of consumer activism serves as a means of expressing discontent or disagreement with a nation's policies, practices, or values. By refraining from buying products tied to the targeted nation, proponents of nationalist boycotts aim to exert economic pressure and create an impact on the nation's economy. This type of PCN can be seen as a form of protest or resistance, leveraging consumer choices to convey a political message. In contrast, the second subtype of PCN, nationalist buycotts, centers around encouraging the consumption of domestic goods while deliberately avoiding foreign products in general. This approach is driven by a desire to prioritize and support the domestic economy over foreign competitors. Advocates of nationalist buycotts believe that by favoring domestic products, they can strengthen the nation's economy, protect local industries, and foster a sense of national identity and unity. This type of PCN aims to promote economic self-sufficiency and reduce dependence on foreign markets. By distinguishing between nationalist boycotts and nationalist buycotts, Castello provides a nuanced understanding of the diverse strategies employed within the realm of PCN. These subtypes highlight the range of motivations and actions adopted by individuals or groups engaging in political consumerism. Whether it is refusing to purchase products associated with a specific nation or actively supporting domestic goods, PCN serves as a powerful tool for expressing political opinions and shaping economic dynamics. Castello's refinement of the PCN framework underscores the complexity of consumer nationalism and its implications for both the economy and politics. By recognizing the distinct subtypes of PCN, researchers and policymakers can better analyze and respond to the various ways in which consumers leverage their purchasing power to influence national and international dynamics.

In contrast to PCN, SCN shifts the focus toward cultural objectives rather than overtly political ones. SCN centers on discourses and practices that aim to reinforce nationalism through the act of consuming, using, purchasing, or displaying products and services that are either domestically produced or widely recognized as representing the nation. The primary goal of SCN is to perpetuate and reproduce a sense of national identity through consumer choices. It encompasses a broad range of manifestations, spanning from explicit and deliberate acts such as wearing a T-shirt adorned with a national flag to more subtle and subconscious shopping preferences. These acts of consumption contribute to the construction and reinforcement of nationhood, often through unreflective assumptions and dispositions. As Edensor (2002) argues, the notion of nationhood is partially constituted by everyday performances that may not be immediately recognized as national in nature. These performances occur within a national context and are shaped by unreflexive assumptions and dispositions that evolve within that context. They form part of what Edensor refers to as the "habitus" of a nation, which encompasses the ingrained behaviors, preferences, and practices that reflect national identity (p. 88). By highlighting the role of SCN, researchers delve into the subtle yet influential ways in which individuals contribute to the reproduction of nationalism through their consumption behaviors. From consciously choosing products that are associated with their nation to unconsciously aligning with national values through their mundane shopping habits, consumers participate in the continuous construction and expression of national identity. Understanding the dynamics of SCN provides insight into the complex interplay between consumption, culture, and national belonging. It emphasizes that consumer choices are not solely driven by political motives but also by cultural affiliations and a desire to affirm and express one's national identity. By recognizing the significance of SCN, researchers and observers gain a deeper understanding of how consumer practices intertwine with the formation and perpetuation of nationalism in society.

It is crucial to recognize that SCN extends beyond the consumption of domestically produced goods and services. In fact, SCN can manifest in response to imported commodities, including items that are commonly perceived as thoroughly global in nature. This perspective highlights the power of individual ownership or consumption of goods that are perceived as integral to national culture as a significant mechanism for nation-building. Foster's study of nation-making in Papua New Guinea sheds light on this phenomenon (2002, pp. 63–127). He demonstrates that the individual possession or consumption of goods perceived as emblematic of national culture plays a crucial role in the process of nation-building. This impact is not limited to local commodities such as rice and betel nut but extends to globally recognized products like Coca-Cola. Foster's research challenges the assumption that nation-building is solely dependent on the consumption of locally produced goods. Instead, it emphasizes how the appropriation and integration of global commodities into the fabric of national culture contribute to the construction and reinforcement of national identity. Even seemingly universal products like Coca-Cola can acquire distinct national connotations and become powerful symbols of collective identity. This perspective highlights the complexity of SCN, where consumer choices extend beyond geographic boundaries. Individuals may intentionally align themselves with globally recognized brands or products, perceiving them as representative of their national identity.

Hot consumer nationalism and cold consumer nationalism

The categorization of consumer nationalism discussed earlier builds upon Michael Billig's concept of "hot nationalism" (1995) and expands upon his distinction between banal and "hot" forms of nationalism. Billig's framework highlights the importance of recognizing the taken-for-granted nature of nationalism and national symbols, particularly in the context of established nations. According to Billig, banal nationalism refers to the everyday, mundane ways in which nationalism is reproduced and maintained within a society. It involves the subtle and often unnoticed manifestations of national identity that permeate daily life, such as the display of national flags, the use of national symbols, or the unquestioned acceptance of national narratives. Banal nationalism operates on an unconscious level, becoming an integral part of people's lives and contributing to the sustained reproduction of national identity. In contrast, "hot nationalism" refers to moments of intense national fervor and explicit displays of patriotism, often arising in response to specific events or circumstances. These instances of "hot nationalism" tend to be more visible and overt, capturing public attention and generating heightened emotions. They can be associated with significant political, social, or cultural events that trigger a surge of nationalistic sentiments and expressions. Building upon Billig's framework, the approach of categorizing consumer nationalism discussed earlier acknowledges the banal reproduction of nationalism within established nations. It recognizes that consumer behaviors and choices play a significant role in perpetuating national identity and reinforcing the taken-for-grantedness of nationalism. By understanding how consumer practices contribute to the everyday reproduction of nationalism, researchers gain insights into the complex interplay between consumption, identity, and the enduring presence of national symbols.

Michael Billig's concept of banal nationalism captures the often unnoticed and taken-for-granted signs of nationalism that permeate everyday life. It encompasses ordinary manifestations such as flags displayed on public buildings or the use of deictic words like "ours" or "us" in the media. These seemingly mundane reproductions of the nation play a crucial role in sustaining national identity on a daily basis. The term "banal" in banal nationalism does not imply a sense of naivety. Instead, it underscores the ordinary and pervasive nature of nationalist symbols and discourses that become deeply ingrained in the fabric of society. The banality of nationalism lies in its ability to blend seamlessly into the background of everyday life, where national symbols and narratives are present but often go unnoticed or unquestioned. However, it is precisely this banal reproduction of nationalism that facilitates the mobilization of national sentiments during moments of crisis. When faced with significant challenges or threats, these deeply ingrained symbols and discourses can be quickly activated, evoking a sense of national unity and rallying support for governmental actions or interventions, both domestically and abroad. Billig argues that banal nationalism acts as a foundation upon which "hot nationalism" can be built. "Hot nationalism" refers to the explicit and fervent expressions of national pride and identity that arise in response to specific events or circumstances. Without the groundwork of banal nationalism, the sudden surges of "hot nationalism" would lack the underlying sense of national identity that enables their mobilization and resonance within society. Therefore, the concept of banal nationalism serves as a critical lens for understanding the subtle mechanisms through which national sentiments are reproduced and sustained. It highlights how the ordinary, everyday practices of nationalism contribute to the resilience and mobilization of national identity, playing a vital role in shaping public opinion and support for governmental actions.

In his work *Banal Nationalism* (1995), Michael Billig shed light on an often overlooked aspect of nationalism by highlighting the significance of banal forms of nationalism in well-established Western democratic countries. He conducted a one-day survey of national newspapers in England, using it as a basis to demonstrate the extensive reliance on national symbols and signs within these societies. Billig's analysis challenged the prevailing focus on overt and "hot" manifestations of nationalism, which had traditionally received more attention in academic and scholarly discourse. Typically, nationalist movements seeking secession or regions embroiled in conflict and war were the primary subjects of study when examining nationalism. However, Billig argued that the banal forms of nationalism, the everyday and taken-for-granted expressions of national identity, had been largely overlooked. By examining the contents of national newspapers, Billig revealed how national symbols, narratives, and language permeated the media landscape, reflecting and reinforcing a sense of national identity. These banal manifestations of nationalism, often unremarked and unchallenged, played a significant role in shaping public perceptions and sustaining the nation-state in well-established democratic contexts.

Billig's findings challenged the notion that nationalism was only relevant or worth studying in times of crisis or overt expressions of conflict. Instead, he emphasized that banal nationalism was an inherent and pervasive feature of everyday life in these societies. The quotidian reproduction of nationalism through symbols, signs, and discourses had a subtle yet profound impact on the collective consciousness, contributing to the construction and maintenance of national identity. By bringing attention to the banal forms of nationalism, Billig broadened the scope of nationalist studies and deepened our understanding of the mechanisms through which national identity is sustained. His work highlighted the need to recognize the significance of seemingly ordinary expressions of nationalism in the context of stable, democratic nations, challenging the dominant focus on more visible and intense manifestations of nationalist sentiment.

Therefore, to better understand the complexities of consumer nationalism in China, it is necessary to go beyond the existing categorizations of "hot" and "cold" consumer nationalism, which primarily focus on the explicit and mundane expressions, respectively. While these categorizations capture important aspects of consumer nationalism, they fail to adequately address the consequences of consumer behavior, which form the foundation for the analysis presented in this book. China's unique context presents a distinct set of challenges and dynamics when it comes to consumer nationalism. The interplay between nationalism, consumption, and economic factors in China requires a fresh perspective to comprehensively grasp the phenomenon. Thus, this book proposes a new categorization framework specifically tailored to understanding consumer nationalism in China. This proposed categorization acknowledges the need to bridge the existing gap and offers a more nuanced lens through which to examine consumer nationalism in China. It takes into account the consequences of consumer behavior, recognizing that the choices individuals make as consumers can have wide-ranging impacts on society, the economy, and the nation as a whole.

Chinese Characteristics of Consumer Nationalism

The complexity of Chinese consumer nationalism necessitates a thorough examination of its triggers and underlying causes. By focusing on the consequences of consumer behavior, it becomes possible to gain insight into the factors that drive and shape nationalist sentiments. Therefore, this book proposes a categorization framework for Chinese consumer nationalism based on the associated consequences of such behavior. The proposed categorization takes into account the multifaceted outcomes that arise from consumer nationalist actions in China. By analyzing these consequences, it becomes possible to trace back to the triggers and motivations that drive individuals to engage in nationalist consumption practices. This approach offers a unique perspective on understanding the complex interplay between consumer behavior and nationalism in the Chinese context. The book suggests the following categorization methods to capture the various consequences associated with Chinese consumer nationalism:

1. Carnivalesque participation

   The concept of "Carnival" as coined by Bakhtin in 1984 has gained popularity in post-modern critical circles and has been adapted for literary and semiotic analysis. In these contexts, the term "Carnival" carries subversive connotations, with its laughter and festivities considered as a means of debasing societal norms and hierarchies. When applied to the concept of consumer nationalism, the notion of "Carnivalesque participation" refers to a form of engagement that transcends mere observation and becomes an active, immersive experience. Unlike a spectacle that is passively viewed by the audience, the Carnival blurs the boundaries between art and real life, inviting individuals to partake in its festivities and actively participate. In the context of consumer nationalism, "Carnivalesque participation" involves individuals not only consuming products associated with national identity but also actively engaging in the performances and rituals surrounding those products. It encompasses a sense of lived experience, where individuals become part of the narrative and contribute to the ongoing construction and reproduction of national identity.

   Within the framework of consumer nationalism, "Carnivalesque participation" challenges conventional notions of consumerism by incorporating elements of subversion and playful disruption. It enables individuals to express their nationalist sentiments through acts that go beyond ordinary consumption and delve into the realm of collective celebration and participation. By actively participating in the Carnival of consumer nationalism, individuals not only reinforce their sense of national identity but also challenge established power structures and norms. The laughter and debasement associated with Carnival create a space for temporary liberation, where societal hierarchies can be temporarily overturned, and alternative narratives and voices can emerge.

The concept of "Carnivalesque participation" highlights the transformative potential of consumer nationalism, allowing individuals to actively shape and redefine their national identities. It emphasizes the lived experience and collective engagement that goes beyond the mere act of consumption, inviting individuals to become active participants in the ongoing performance of national belonging. Drawing on Bakhtin's notion of the Carnival, "Carnivalesque participation" offers a framework for understanding the dynamic and interactive nature of consumer nationalism. It recognizes the power of collective celebration, laughter, and subversion in shaping and reimagining national identities, creating spaces where individuals can actively engage and participate in the ongoing construction of their shared cultural and national heritage.

Although Bakhtin initially associated the concept of Carnival with literary modes, its application can extend beyond the realm of literature to encompass various informal occasions of "free" public interactions. In this broader sense, Carnival becomes a lens through which we can understand how people engage in unconventional, subversive behavior within social spaces. These social spaces provide opportunities for conventional power relations to be temporarily overturned and challenged. Through the expression of popular, earthly, and grotesque culture, Carnival allows for the emergence of a wildly funny and transformative experience. It serves as a platform where individuals can explore and reconcile the tension between utopian ideals and the realities of everyday life. By embracing a Carnivalesque approach, people navigate their way through discussions and resolutions of social issues. They adopt a mode of expression characterized by humor, irony, and satire, allowing them to engage with sensitive topics in a playful and subversive manner. This approach not only offers a means of catharsis and collective enjoyment but also serves as a strategy for coping with the complexities of social life.

One example of Carnivalesque behavior in the context of consumer nationalism is the phenomenon of anti-CNN nationalism in China. The "C gesture" emerged as a symbol of resistance against perceived biased media coverage by the international news network CNN. In response to what some individuals viewed as unfavorable reporting about China, people creatively employed the "C gesture," which involved making a thumb and forefinger circle while holding up the remaining three fingers to symbolize "Chinese" and imply a derogatory connotation toward CNN. This Carnivalesque gesture served as a form of protest and humorously challenged the authority and credibility of CNN. It provided a means for individuals to express their frustrations and discontent in a lighthearted yet powerful way, utilizing symbolism and satire to navigate and address perceived biases in media representation. By analyzing such examples of Carnivalesque behavior, we gain insight into the strategies individuals employ to negotiate social issues within a playful and subversive framework. The Carnivalesque allows for the temporary suspension of established norms, encouraging dialogue, critique, and a reimagining of power dynamics. It offers a space where alternative narratives can emerge and provide a sense of empowerment and collective identity.

2. Rational resistance

The second type of Chinese consumer nationalism can be characterized as "rational resistance." Unlike emotional or impulsive forms of consumer nationalism, this type involves strategic and calculated boycotts with a clear desired outcome. In the context of rational resistance, Chinese consumers carefully analyze their purchasing decisions and actively choose to boycott certain products or brands based on specific reasons. These reasons may include political controversies, territorial disputes, perceived threats to national security, or concerns about the ethical practices of foreign companies. What sets rational resistance apart is its deliberate and calculated nature. Consumers engage in a thoughtful assessment of the consequences of their actions and seek to achieve tangible results through their boycotts. They consider the potential impact on the targeted companies or countries and aim to exert pressure or influence them to align with Chinese interests or values. This rational approach is characterized by a clear strategic objective and a rational cost-benefit analysis. Consumers evaluate the potential benefits of their boycotts, such as sending a strong message of solidarity and nationalism, protecting domestic industries, or influencing policy changes. They also weigh the potential costs, such as the availability of alternative products, the potential economic repercussions, and the effectiveness of their collective action. Rational resistance reflects a calculated form of consumer nationalism where individuals seek to leverage their economic power to achieve specific goals. It is based on the understanding that consumer choices have the potential to shape market dynamics and impact the behavior of targeted entities. By engaging in rational resistance, Chinese consumers aim to assert their national identity, protect national interests, and promote their values through targeted boycotts. They use their consumer choices as a means of expressing dissent, exerting influence, and achieving desired outcomes that align with their vision of a stronger and more prosperous China.

An example of rational consumer nationalism in China is the "Buy Chinese" movement. This movement encourages Chinese consumers to prioritize and support domestic products over foreign alternatives. It promotes the idea that by purchasing Chinese-made goods, individuals are contributing to the growth of the national economy, fostering domestic industries, and asserting national pride. The "Buy Chinese" movement emerged in response to concerns about the country's reliance on foreign products and the perceived impact on domestic industries and employment. It aims to bolster the competitiveness of Chinese brands and promote the consumption of locally produced goods. Rational consumer nationalism comes into play as individuals make conscious and informed choices to support domestic products based on considerations such as quality, affordability, and economic impact. It is driven by the rationale that by buying Chinese-made products, consumers are not only fulfilling their own needs but also actively contributing to the welfare and development of their country. This rational approach to consumer nationalism emphasizes the importance of economic factors and the desire to strengthen the nation's industrial base. It is grounded in the belief that supporting domestic industries through consumption can lead to increased economic self-reliance, technological advancement, and global competitiveness.

3. Vigilantism

The third type of Chinese consumer nationalism can be categorized as "vigilantism," as it involves consumers engaging in irrational and often disruptive behaviors without clear goals or realistic end results in mind. This form of consumer nationalism is characterized by impulsive actions driven by heightened emotions and a desire to express outrage or assert nationalistic fervor. Vigilante consumer nationalists often display a lack of rationality and foresight in their behavior. Their actions may include participating in protests, engaging in acts of violence or vandalism, or resorting to extreme measures to express their discontent with a particular country or brand. These actions can extend to targeting individuals and property associated with the perceived "enemy," such as drivers of Japanese cars in the case of anti-Japan protests. The language and actions associated with vigilantism in consumer nationalism are typically disruptive and confrontational. Participants may employ inflammatory rhetoric, engage in acts of aggression, or contribute to an atmosphere of hostility. The primary focus is on expressing anger and asserting a sense of nationalistic identity, often without a clear understanding of how these actions will contribute to achieving meaningful change or resolving the underlying issues. It is important to note that vigilantism within consumer nationalism often lacks a well-defined set of goals or a realistic understanding of the consequences of their actions. The behavior is driven by strong emotions and a desire to retaliate against perceived injustices or affronts to the nation's pride. However, the outcomes sought may be unrealistic or disconnected from the actual issues at hand.

Instances of anti-Japan protests leading to the beating of drivers of Japanese cars and damaging vehicles exemplify the vigilantism aspect of Chinese consumer nationalism. In such cases, individuals may vent their anger toward symbols associated with a particular country or brand without considering the broader implications of their actions. The behaviors displayed are impulsive and often fueled by a desire to exact immediate retribution or assert dominance. In summary, the concept of vigilantism within Chinese consumer nationalism refers to irrational and disruptive behaviors driven by heightened emotions and a lack of clear goals. Participants engage in impulsive actions that may not align with realistic expectations or contribute to meaningful change. The language and actions associated with vigilantism tend to be confrontational and disruptive, with a focus on expressing anger and asserting nationalistic identity rather than achieving tangible outcomes.

Conclusion

This chapter takes a fresh and alternative approach to the examination of consumer nationalism in China. Rather than relying on the conventional categorization of nationalistic behaviors, this chapter proposes a new framework that focuses on the motivations driving consumer nationalism and the resulting consequences of these actions. By shifting the emphasis from specific behaviors to the underlying motivations and outcomes, this approach seeks to provide a more nuanced understanding of Chinese consumer nationalism. It recognizes that consumer nationalist actions can stem from a variety of motivations and can lead to diverse consequences, both intended and unintended. The proposed framework acknowledges that consumer nationalist behaviors in China are not monolithic but rather multifaceted and complex. It recognizes that individuals may be motivated by various factors such as economic considerations, national pride, political ideologies, or concerns about domestic industries and employment. These motivations can shape the nature and intensity of their consumer nationalist actions.

Additionally, this approach highlights the significance of examining the consequences of consumer nationalist actions. It recognizes that these actions can have far-reaching effects on various stakeholders, including businesses, economies, international relations, and even individuals within the nation itself. By examining the consequences, the chapter aims to shed light on the potential impacts, both positive and negative, that arise from consumer nationalism in China. This alternative approach also acknowledges the dynamic nature of consumer nationalism and the evolving landscape of Chinese society. It recognizes that motivations and consequences can change over time and in response to social, economic, and political developments. By focusing on these dynamic aspects, the chapter seeks to capture the complexity and fluidity of consumer nationalism in China. In summary, this chapter adopts a fresh perspective on the examination of consumer nationalism in China by categorizing it based on motivations and consequences. By doing so, it aims to provide a deeper understanding of the diverse motivations that drive consumer nationalist actions and the varied outcomes that result from these actions. This alternative approach acknowledges the multifaceted nature of consumer nationalism and the dynamic nature of Chinese society, contributing to a more comprehensive understanding of this complex phenomenon.

Chapter 5

GROWING RISK FOR MULTINATIONAL BUSINESSES

This chapter argues that China's emergence as the world's number two economy presenting complexities for multinational businesses to navigate. Drawing on the author's own experience in training multinational businesses in China, the chapter highlights the rising tide of nationalistic sentiment in recent years, which has led to heightened outrage toward foreign brands for perceived offenses against China and Chinese interests. This wave of nationalism has reached a fever pitch, resulting in a climate of extreme caution among many multinational firms, including certain Chinese domestic companies that have partnered with foreign brands. As a result, these companies find themselves navigating a complex landscape when operating in the world's second-largest economy. They face pressures from various quarters, including the Chinese government's increasingly nationalistic stance, which seeks to tighten its governance and exert a direct role in business operations.

History of Multinational Business Development in China

China, as one of the world's largest economies, has emerged as a highly attractive investment destination for numerous multinational companies (MNCs), both Western and from other regions. Since its opening up in 1979 and the subsequent adoption of free market principles, China has experienced remarkable economic growth and transformation, becoming a prominent player on the global stage. Its vast market, abundant resources, and skilled workforce have made it an enticing prospect for businesses seeking growth and expansion opportunities. Over the years, China has established itself as a hub for manufacturing, technology, and services, attracting investments from a wide range of industries. The country's favorable business environment, improved infrastructure, and government initiatives to promote foreign investment have further contributed to its status as one of the world's most well-known and sought-after investment destinations.

However, the history of multinational business development in China extends far beyond the recent decades. In fact, it can be traced back to the late nineteenth century when foreign firms first set their sights on establishing a presence in the country. At that time, China's vast market and untapped potential presented an alluring opportunity for MNCs seeking avenues for growth and expansion. These early endeavors were primarily driven by the desire to access the Chinese market and cater to its burgeoning consumer base. The early twentieth century posed significant challenges for foreign firms operating in China. Political instability, the Chinese Civil War, and the economic turmoil caused by the First World War disrupted business operations and hindered multinational growth. However, despite these setbacks, the growth of MNCs in China regained momentum after the Second World War. Following the war, China underwent significant political and economic transformations, including the establishment of the People's Republic of China in 1949.

The subsequent period of economic reform and opening up in 1979 brought renewed opportunities for foreign businesses to engage with China. The Chinese government's efforts to attract foreign investment and promote economic development paved the way for MNCs to reestablish and expand their presence in the country. Since then, multinational corporations from various parts of the world have flocked to China, drawn by its immense market potential, abundant resources, and skilled labor force. The country's economic rise and integration into the global economy have further solidified its appeal as a strategic investment destination. Today, China stands as a vital hub for multinational operations, serving as a crucial market, production base, and research and development center for countless global corporations.

During the 1960s and 1970s, China had limited opportunities for foreign investment, and its economy remained largely closed off to MNCs. However, a turning point emerged in the late 1970s when China embarked on a transformative journey of economic openness and market-oriented reforms. Consequently, multinational corporations seized the opportunity to establish a foothold in China and capitalize on its expanding market and comparatively lower labor costs. Throughout the 1980s and 1990s, multinational enterprises experienced rapid growth as they expanded their operations in China. Many companies chose to relocate their manufacturing facilities to leverage the country's cost advantages in terms of labor. Simultaneously, China persisted in implementing economic reforms and further opening its doors to foreign investment, intensifying the attractiveness of the Chinese market for multinational corporations.

During the early stage of China's opening up, there were around 100 foreign companies in China. This figure went up 28 times in less than two decades. In 1998, the number of foreign-owned enterprises in China was 280,000; U.S. companies had the biggest investment, including General Motors, Motorola, General Electric, Arco, Coca-Cola, Hewlett-Packard, Proctor & Gamble, Amoco, and United Technologies. Overall, foreign companies doing business in China are required to form joint ventures with Chinese companies instead of forming wholly owned subsidiaries. Due to the concerns that foreign companies might take over entire sectors of the economy, entrance by foreign companies to the Chinese market is often determined by how much technology and how much benefit the foreign company could potentially bring to the country.

From 1979 to 2019, MNCs experienced a progressively open and favorable business environment in China, characterized by unhindered capital flows, trade, and the exchange of ideas (McKinsey, 2023). This environment facilitated the establishment of global supply chains and catered to the demands of an increasingly interconnected world. Notably, American MNCs such as Yum! Brands (YUM), the parent company of popular chains like Pizza Hut, KFC, and Taco Bell, witnessed rapid expansion within China. Over the course of a decade from 2009 to 2019, Pizza Hut's franchises doubled, McDonald's Corp. presently operates over 3,700 locations in China as of 2020, and Starbucks experienced significant growth, boasting 5,000 stores in 200 cities across mainland China. Additionally, numerous non-Western MNCs have established a presence in China. For instance, Japanese automakers such as Toyota, Mitsubishi, and Subaru, as well as Korean industry giants like Samsung, Hyundai, LG (Lucky Goldstar), and Kia, have invested in the country's market.

During the period characterized by relatively more openness and freedom, two significant factors emerged. First, it becomes apparent that Japanese companies faced heightened scrutiny compared to Chinese companies or those from other nations. This scrutiny encompassed both Japanese products and advertising campaigns by Japanese companies. The rationale behind this phenomenon is rather straightforward: the existence of anti-Japanese sentiments in China, largely stemming from the historical conflicts between the two nations, specifically the Sino-Japanese wars in 1931 and 1937, as well as the dispute over Diaoyu Island. A notable example occurred in 2012 when Japanese automakers like Toyota and Honda were adversely affected by Chinese boycotts following Japan's decision to nationalize the contested island, known as Senkaku in Japan.

Another noteworthy factor is the requirement for American companies conducting business in China to provide assurance to the United States government that their operations will not pose any threats to American national security. In 2006, the Chinese government imposed restrictions on real-estate investment and implemented stricter controls on mergers involving foreign companies. As a result, The Carlyle Group's attempt to acquire 85 percent of Xugong, the largest manufacturer of construction equipment in China, was ultimately abandoned.

This summarizes two important elements in understanding the circumstances of MNCs' operation in China: (1) nationalism's impact and (2) potential conflicts of national interests. Understanding the existence of these two factors and their impact on doing business in China is essential for the interpretation of and preparation for the current risks for MNCs operating in China. And these two elements will be analyzed in the later sections.

Although 2,800 exhibitors from 145 countries recently turned up to flog their wares at the China International Import Expo in Shanghai in 2022, in aggregate global business' exposure to China looks modest (Economist, 2022). In a world reshaped by rising geopolitical tensions, renewed inflationary pressures, impact of COVID pandemic, and in a country where some of the most dramatic reconfigurations may take place, MNCs are reassessing, re-evaluating, and reconfiguring their businesses for a new era and their operations in China. According to McKinsey Global Institute's most recent report published in January 2023 titled "the China imperative for multinational companies," Multinational corporations (MNCs) are currently reevaluating their ties with China. According to a recent survey, the percentage of U.S. MNCs considering China among their top three investment priorities declined from 77 percent in 2010 to 45 percent in 2022. While several MNCs are still actively investing in China, some are scaling back their operations or redistributing their investments to other nations. A few are even opting to withdraw entirely from China. These adjustments are occurring amidst the ongoing challenges presented by the COVID-19 pandemic and increased economic tensions between China and the United States, multinationals remain attracted to China's large market, growing middle class, and expanding technological capabilities, and many companies are looking to increase their presence in the country in the years to come (McKinsey, 2023).

China's Economic Role in the World

China, being one of the largest economies globally, holds a prominent position in the global economic landscape. Its significant role as a major exporter and manufacturer contributes significantly to international trade and has been instrumental in driving global economic growth. Furthermore, China's extensive investments in infrastructure and development projects in various nations through the Belt and Road Initiative have further solidified its influence. However, China's position in the world economy has sparked debates and controversies. Some argue that its state-led economic model and trade practices pose challenges to the global trade system. Conversely, others view China's economic ascent as a potential source of new opportunities and a catalyst for global economic growth. It is important to recognize that China's economic role on the global stage is intricate and multifaceted, and its impact on the global economy is expected to undergo further transformation in the years to come.

In their insightful book *China's Rise: Challenges and Opportunities* published in 2009, Bergsten, Freeman, Lardy, and Mitchell shed light on the multifaceted impact of China's rise on the United States and the global community. They emphasize that China's emergence presents both challenges and opportunities that demand careful consideration. Understanding the nature and implications of China's ascent is crucial as the United States and other nations gear up to confront these challenges and capitalize on the potential opportunities that lie ahead. It is imperative to approach this task with clarity and objectivity, ensuring a comprehensive grasp of the complexities involved. China's rise has undoubtedly introduced a new dynamic in global affairs, affecting various aspects such as economics, politics, and security. The sheer scale of China's economy, its growing influence in international trade, and its expanding global footprint necessitate a strategic approach to navigating the evolving dynamics of the U.S.-China relationship.

China's rapid economic growth and its status as the world's second-largest economy have led to debates about its impact on other countries, especially developed economies. China's economic rise has fueled competition with the United States, particularly in the technology and manufacturing sectors. China is a major trade partner with Europe, and its growth has led to increased competition in a variety of industries, including automobiles and consumer goods. China's rise has had a significant impact on Japan's economy, particularly in the manufacturing sector. China's economic growth has led to increased competition with other Asian countries, particularly in the manufacturing and export industries. China's growth has also led to increased competition with other emerging economies, such as India, Brazil, and Russia. These economic competitions can have implications for trade relations, investment flows, and the overall balance of power in the global economy.

China's trade policies, particularly with regard to intellectual property rights, have led to tensions with other countries, including the United States. China has had trade tensions with several countries and regions around the world. The United States and China have been involved in a trade war since 2018, with both countries imposing tariffs on each other's goods. The

tensions stem from disagreements over trade imbalances, intellectual property theft, and technology transfer. China and Europe have had tensions
over issues such as steel overcapacity and investment restrictions, leading to
increased scrutiny of Chinese investment in Europe. China and Japan have
had trade tensions in the past, particularly over the Senkaku Islands dispute
and Japan's trade policies with China. China has had trade tensions with
several Southeast Asian countries over territorial disputes in the South China
Sea. Australia and China have had trade tensions in recent years, particularly
over issues such as Australian criticism of China's human rights record and
Australia's ban on Huawei's participation in its 5G network. These trade tensions can have a significant impact on global trade and investment flows and
can result in economic and geopolitical consequences for all parties involved.

Debates center around China's currency manipulation, which refers to
the accusation that China artificially lowers the value of its currency, the
Renminbi (also known as the Yuan), to make its exports cheaper and more
competitive on the global market. Critics of China's currency practices argue
that the manipulation gives Chinese businesses an unfair advantage and contributes to the trade imbalances between China and its trading partners, such
as the United States. This has led to calls for China to allow its currency to
float freely on international markets, which would be determined by market
forces rather than government intervention.

China has long maintained that its currency practices are within the
bounds of international law and that it has not engaged in systematic manipulation. The Chinese government has taken steps in recent years to allow
greater flexibility in the exchange rate of the Renminbi, but it still exercises
significant control over the currency's value. The issue of currency manipulation remains a contentious one in international trade, with many countries
and organizations accusing China of unfair practices and calling for greater
exchange rate transparency and reform.

Critics also argue that China's markets are not sufficiently open to foreign
investment and competition, while proponents argue that China has made
significant progress in recent years.

They argue that the country's state-led economic model and restrictions
on foreign investment limit the full potential of its market. Critics argue that
China does not adequately protect the intellectual property rights of foreign
companies operating in the country, leading to widespread infringement and
theft of patents and trademarks. Many foreign companies are required to
transfer technology to their Chinese partners as a condition for entering the
Chinese market, which critics argue is a form of intellectual property theft.

Critics also argue that China's state-owned enterprises receive unfair
advantages and subsidies, giving them an edge over private and foreign-owned

firms in the domestic market. Foreign investment is often restricted in sensitive industries, such as technology and media, which limits the ability of foreign companies to fully participate in the Chinese market. Companies operating in China face a range of regulatory barriers and obstacles to market access, such as discriminatory regulations and licensing requirements.

These criticisms suggest that China's market openness is limited and that the country's state-led economic model provides significant advantages to domestic companies, hindering the potential of its market and creating an uneven playing field for foreign businesses.

In addition, there are ongoing debates about China's human rights record and labor standards, with some arguing that these issues pose a risk to foreign investment and economic relations with other countries. China has faced criticism and concerns over labor standards in recent years; critics argue that, despite the country's economic growth, wages for many workers in China remain low, and there have been reports of widespread wage theft and nonpayment of wages. China has a large manufacturing sector, and there have been widespread reports of dangerous working conditions, long hours, and inadequate safety measures in many factories. Other concerns include that Chinese workers do not have the same rights and protections as workers in many other countries, and there have been reports of widespread abuses of workers' rights, including forced labor and repression of workers who attempt to form unions or protest working conditions. There have been reports of widespread health and safety violations in China's workplaces, including exposure to hazardous chemicals and pollutants, as well as inadequate provision of personal protective equipment.

These labor standards debates have raised concerns among international consumers and businesses, leading to calls for greater protections for workers in China and greater transparency in the country's labor practices. Some businesses have also taken steps to improve labor standards in their supply chains by implementing codes of conduct and monitoring programs.

Overall, these debates have implications for the global economy and for the future of China's role in the world. China has had a significant impact on the global economy in recent decades, becoming one of the world's largest economies and a major player in international trade and investment. China's rapid economic growth has driven global economic growth, with the country becoming a major market for goods and services from around the world.

China is the world's largest exporter, and its trade relationships with other countries have significant implications for the global economy. The country's growing middle class and its increasing consumption of goods and services have also driven demand for imports from around the world. China has become a major source of foreign investment for many countries, investing in infrastructure, real estate, and other assets around the world.

The value of China's currency, the Renminbi (also known as the Yuan), has a significant impact on the global economy, with fluctuations in its value affecting exchange rates and trade flows around the world. China's rise as a major economic power has led to increased competition in many industries, with Chinese companies challenging established players in many markets around the world. China's impact on the global economy has been significant, with the country becoming a major driver of economic growth and a key player in international trade and investment. Its continued economic development and integration into the global economy will likely shape the future of the global economy in the years to come.

Breslin's (2005) article, "Power and Production: Rethinking China's Global Economic Role," intends to highlight that although China holds considerable importance for the global and East Asian economies, the magnitude of its economic influence may not be as extensive as suggested by headline figures. The significant disparity between China being one of the largest economies globally and still classified as a relatively poor economy poses a crucial challenge. However, this challenge prompts a distinct set of policy considerations, diverging from the perception of China as an economic superpower. The article anticipates that China might deviate from the developmental path observed in countries such as Japan and South Korea.

The future of China's role in the world is therefore also a subject of much debate and speculation. Some of the key factors that are likely to shape China's future role in the world include economic growth, political and military power, diplomatic relationships, domestic developments, and technological advancement. China's continued economic growth will likely play a major role in shaping the country's future role in the world. A continued period of strong growth would likely increase China's influence and its ability to shape global economic and political developments. China's growing political and military power will also play a significant role in shaping the country's future role in the world. As China becomes more assertive on the international stage, it is likely to challenge the dominant role of the United States and other established powers in shaping global affairs.

China's relationships with other countries, particularly its major trading partners, will also play a significant role in shaping its future role in the world. As China continues to build relationships with other countries, it is likely to become increasingly influential in regional and global affairs. Domestic developments in China, including economic and social reforms, will also play a role in shaping the country's future role in the world. Changes to China's political system, such as increased political liberalization, could have significant implications for the country's future role in the world. China's continued technological advancement, particularly in areas such as artificial intelligence and 5G, is also likely to play a role in shaping the country's future role in the world.

Given these factors and the many uncertainties surrounding the future, it is difficult to predict exactly what China's role in the world will be in the years to come. However, it is likely that China will continue to play a significant role in shaping global economic and political developments, and its influence will likely continue to grow in the coming years. As Bergsten et al. (2009) conclude, China's rise provides the United States and global community with a great number of both challenges and opportunities. As the United States and others prepare to meet those challenges and seize those opportunities, it will be crucial to have a clear and objective understanding of the nature and implications of China's emergence.

As Hang (2017) summarizes in his article, the rise of China may challenge the United States as well as underline the implications and options for the United States. Based on a thorough analysis of developments in China's path to become a powerhouse on the world stage, namely China's economic success, military modernization, increased soft power in Asia and around the globe, and China's ambition to have an influential role in the international system, Hang (2017) employs the Hegemonic Cycle framework to establish empirical evidence of the rise and decline of the world powers since the sixteenth century. Applying this to the case of China's rise and the United States as a lonely superpower in the contemporary world politics, Hang (2017) demonstrates that the United States needs to be prepared to both cooperate and confront with China.

Political Implications and Growing Risk

The emergence of China as the world's second-largest economy has brought about significant political consequences both within its borders and on the global scale. Domestically, this economic growth has resulted in improved living standards and overall economic progress. However, it has also accentuated social and economic disparities, leading to heightened inequalities among different segments of society. On the international front, China's rise has granted the country enhanced political and economic influence, positioning it as a prominent player in global affairs. China has displayed a more assertive approach in pursuing its national interests, exerting its power and shaping international dynamics. Nevertheless, this growing influence has raised concerns among other nations, particularly in relation to trade and territorial disputes, which have introduced complexities and tensions into global relationships. China's ascendance as the world's second-largest economy has triggered notable political ramifications at home and abroad. While it has brought about positive changes, such as economic growth, it has also given rise to disparities and intensified global concerns. The intricacies of China's political system and diplomatic relations further complicate the aspirations of multinational businesses operating in this dynamic environment.

Nationalistic outrage toward foreign brands in China has become an increasingly prevalent trend in recent years. This surge of nationalistic sentiment is frequently fueled by a strong sense of patriotism and a desire to promote and uphold domestic businesses and products. When perceived national interests or sovereignty come under scrutiny or face potential threats, this sentiment intensifies, leading to heightened levels of outrage. The motivations behind this nationalistic outrage are multifaceted. On one hand, there is a genuine desire to support and bolster China's own industries, fostering economic growth and self-reliance. Additionally, this sentiment is driven by a collective belief that by rejecting foreign brands and products, China can assert its independence, assertiveness, and cultural identity on the global stage. It is important to note that while nationalistic outrage toward foreign brands can have significant implications for multinational businesses operating in China, it does not reflect the sentiments of the entire population. Many Chinese consumers still value the quality, reputation, and innovation associated with international brands and continue to engage with them.

The expression of this nationalism can take various forms, such as boycotts of foreign brands or calls for consumers to buy domestic alternatives. Some foreign companies operating in China have faced public backlash and negative publicity, leading them to adopt more local-friendly policies or to apologize for perceived missteps. These expressions of nationalism are an example of how politics and economics are intertwined in China and how they can have a significant impact on the business environment.

Situating in the bigger context, the country's economy is subject to fluctuations and uncertainty, including changes in growth rate, currency value, and trade policies. Intellectual property rights protection remains a challenge for many foreign companies operating in China, and businesses must navigate a complex legal system to enforce their rights. The Chinese market is highly competitive, and companies must adapt to local consumers' preferences and changing market conditions. The complex relationship between China and the international community can lead to geopolitical tensions and economic sanctions, which can disrupt business operations. Negative publicity, such as controversies over labor practices or environmental impact, can damage a company's reputation and impact its business in China. Foreign companies operating in China face strict data privacy regulations and must navigate cultural differences in attitudes toward data privacy and security.

For example, Apple Inc. faced criticism and backlash from Chinese consumers and state media over its warranty policy in early 2013, leading the company to change its practices to better align with local regulations and consumer expectations. Tesla faced production disruptions due to the COVID-19 pandemic and faced competition from local electric vehicle manufacturers in early 2020, leading the company to invest in local production and manufacturing in China. Starbucks faced criticism over its pricing strategy in China in 2011, leading the company to adjust its prices and improve its public relations efforts to better connect with local consumers. Marriott faced significant backlash in 2018 and was forced to apologize over a customer survey that listed Tibet, Hong Kong, Macau, and Taiwan as separate countries, which was perceived as a violation of China's territorial integrity. Google faced significant challenges in re-entering the Chinese market in 2010 due to concerns over data privacy and censorship, leading the company to develop a censored search engine for the market.

These are just a few examples of the risks that foreign businesses can face when operating in China and demonstrate the importance of understanding the local market and political environment in order to be successful in the country. These events took place in recent years and highlight the complex and dynamic business environment in China and the importance of being aware of and responsive to changing local conditions and regulations.

Among all these risks, nationalism in China has had a significant impact on foreign brands operating in the country. On one hand, expressions of nationalism can result in a strong preference for domestic brands and products, leading to increased competition for foreign companies. Nationalistic outrage can also lead to boycotts of foreign brands or negative publicity, damaging a company's reputation and affecting its business in China. On the other hand, some foreign companies have tried to use expressions of nationalism to their advantage by aligning themselves with Chinese patriotism and highlighting their commitment to the market. Foreign brands that are perceived as being respectful of Chinese culture and sensitive to local concerns are more likely to be successful in the market.

In recent years, nationalism has become an increasingly important factor for foreign companies operating in China, and they must be aware of and responsive to these sentiments in order to be successful in the market. Businesses must also be aware of the changing political environment and be prepared to adapt their strategies as needed to succeed in the country.

As of July 1, 2023, the updated China Anti-Espionage Law has taken effect, causing significant concern among foreign business communities in China. This new law is part of a series of 15n national security-related laws implemented in recent years to bolster China's security measures. Under the revised law, the definition of espionage in China has been dramatically expanded, raising potential risks for both companies and individuals. Now, engaging in what were once considered regular business activities may result in penalties if Chinese authorities perceive them as espionage or linked to foreign sanctions against China.

The scope of espionage has broadened considerably, encompassing the unauthorized acquisition of any documents, data, materials, or items related to national security and interests. Previously, the law focused only on "state secrets and intelligence," whereas now, it includes all information vital for national security protection.

Notably, the law does not clearly define the terms "national security" and "interests," leaving room for interpretation and uncertainty. Espionage is now defined as collaborating with spy organizations and their agents, as well as conducting cyber-attacks against state entities, confidential-related units, or critical information infrastructure. Additionally, joining espionage organizations and their agents is now categorized as an espionage activity, without specifying the criteria for such associations.

Moreover, actions such as "inciting," "enticing," "bribing," and "coercing" foreign officials to defect are also considered espionage activities under the updated law.

Given the broad and vague provisions of the law, analysts fear that it might be applied to regular business practices, raising apprehension among foreign businesses operating in China (Jill Goldenziel, 2023).

Systematic Analysis of Recent Triggers

The triggers of nationalism in China are diverse and influenced by historical, geopolitical, cultural, and social factors. Territorial disputes, historical memories, geopolitical tensions, challenges to cultural identity, perceived threats to national interests, and the amplifying effect of social media all contribute to the rise of nationalistic sentiments in the country. After extensively reviewing nearly 50 cases of consumer nationalism in China spanning from 2016 to 2021, several common triggers of nationalist sentiments have emerged. These triggers shed light on the complex and multifaceted nature of nationalism in the Chinese context. Understanding these factors is crucial for comprehending the dynamics that contribute to the rise of nationalistic outrage in the country and is essential for businesses operating in China to navigate the complex landscape of consumer nationalism and effectively engage with the Chinese market. They are summarized as follows:

• Perceived threats to national sovereignty

Issues such as territorial disputes, perceived interference in China's domestic affairs, or challenges to China's political and economic interests can trigger strong nationalist sentiments. One example of this is the controversy surrounding the South China Sea territorial dispute, which has led to nationalist sentiments and calls for the protection of China's territorial interests. The South China Sea territorial dispute has been a source of tensions between China and several neighboring countries for many years. In recent years, this dispute has become more politically charged, leading to increased nationalist sentiments in China. In 2016, an international tribunal ruled that China's claims in the South China Sea were not valid, which led to widespread nationalist reactions, including calls for the protection of China's territorial interests and sovereignty. This issue has continued to be a source of tension and a trigger for nationalist sentiments in China.

• Controversies involving foreign companies

Negative publicity, such as labor disputes, environmental controversies, or incidents involving foreign companies that are perceived as being disrespectful to China or its culture, can trigger expressions of nationalism and lead to boycotts of foreign brands. A well-known example of this is the controversy surrounding Starbucks' comments on the South China Sea dispute, which led to widespread boycott threats and nationalist reactions from consumers and the public. In 2016, Starbucks CEO Howard Schultz made comments about the South China Sea dispute, which were perceived as taking sides against China. These comments led to widespread boycott threats and nationalist reactions from consumers and the public, who saw Starbucks' statements as a threat to China's sovereignty and territorial integrity. This controversy serves as an example of how foreign companies can trigger nationalist sentiments in China if they are perceived to be involved in political issues or controversies.

• Economic concerns

During times of economic uncertainty, such as economic slowdowns or trade tensions, nationalist sentiments can be heightened and expressed through calls to support domestic businesses and products. During the height of the U.S.-China trade tensions in 2018, nationalist sentiments were heightened, leading to calls for support of domestic businesses and products, as well as expressions of economic nationalism. In 2018, the U.S.-China trade tensions heightened, leading to a trade war between the two countries. This economic uncertainty and the potential for economic damage to China led to increased nationalist sentiments, including calls for support of domestic businesses and products and expressions of economic nationalism. The U.S.-China trade tensions served as a trigger for nationalist sentiments in China and demonstrated the impact that economic concerns can have on nationalist sentiments.

- **Political events**

Nationalist sentiments can be triggered by political events, such as the commemoration of important historical events, or during periods of political tensions with foreign countries. For example, the commemoration of the 80th anniversary of the Nanking massacre in 2017 led to heightened nationalist sentiments and calls for the protection of China's national dignity and territorial integrity. This event serves as an example of how political events can trigger nationalist sentiments in China, and how historical events and national traumas can shape contemporary nationalist dynamics.

- **Perceived cultural insensitivity**

Foreign companies that are perceived as being culturally insensitive or disrespectful of Chinese values can trigger expressions of nationalism and negative reactions from consumers and the public. The controversy surrounding Dolce & Gabbana's comments on Chinese culture and customs in 2018 is a well-known example of this trigger, which led to widespread boycott threats and expressions of nationalist sentiments from consumers and the public. In 2018, fashion brand Dolce & Gabbana was caught up in a controversy over comments made about Chinese culture and customs that were perceived as culturally insensitive. The controversy led to widespread boycott threats and expressions of nationalist sentiments from consumers and the public, who saw Dolce & Gabbana's comments as a threat to China's cultural identity and national dignity. This example demonstrates the impact that perceived cultural insensitivity can have on nationalist sentiments in China.

- **National pride and patriotism**

Celebrations of China's achievements and progress can also trigger expressions of nationalism and a strong sense of national pride and patriotism. The celebration of the 70th anniversary of the founding of the People's Republic of China in 2019 is an example of this trigger, where nationalist sentiments were heightened and national pride and patriotism were expressed through events, media, and online activism. In 2019, the 70th anniversary of the founding of the People's Republic of China was celebrated, which led to heightened nationalist sentiments and the expression of national pride and patriotism through events, media, and online activism. This event serves as an example of how celebrations and cultural events can trigger nationalist sentiments in China and how national pride and patriotism can shape nationalist dynamics.

- **Social media and online activism**

The rise of social media and online activism has made it easier for nationalist sentiments to be expressed and amplified, leading to more widespread and impactful expressions of nationalism. The controversy surrounding the 2019 National Basketball Association (NBA) Hong Kong protests is a well-known example of how social media and online activism can trigger nationalist sentiments and lead to widespread calls for a boycott of foreign brands and products. In 2019, the NBA was caught up in a controversy over a statement made in support of the protests in Hong Kong. The controversy led to widespread calls for a boycott of foreign brands and products and nationalist reactions from consumers and the public, who saw the NBA's statement as a threat to China's sovereignty and territorial integrity. This example demonstrates the impact that social media and online activism can have on nationalist sentiments in China and how these dynamics can trigger nationalist reactions.

These are some of the key triggers of nationalism in China, and businesses must be aware of these factors and take them into consideration when operating in the country. Nationalist sentiments can change rapidly and can have a significant impact on a company's reputation and business operations, making it important for companies to be proactive and responsive to these dynamics.

Conclusion

In the past decade, the operating environment for multinational firms in China has undergone significant changes, necessitating a heightened awareness of emerging concerns. To successfully navigate this evolving landscape, foreign brands must recognize the areas that are generating growing apprehension. Operating with caution has become imperative for companies, including Chinese domestic firms that collaborate with certain foreign brands, as they engage with the world's second-largest economy. The forthcoming chapter will delve into practical strategies for managing these risks effectively. It will explore the various dimensions of risk management, offering insights and rec-ommendations to help multinational businesses mitigate potential challenges and capitalize on opportunities. By understanding the evolving dynamics of China's business landscape and proactively addressing areas of concern, com-panies can enhance their chances of success and maintain positive relation-ships with Chinese consumers, stakeholders, and regulatory authorities. The forthcoming chapter aims to equip multinational firms operating in China with actionable insights and best practices. It will empower businesses to nav-igate the complexities of the Chinese market, effectively manage risks, and seize the vast opportunities that China's dynamic economy offers.

Chapter 6

MANAGING RISKS (CONSUMER NATIONALISM RESILIENCE SCALE)

This chapter adopts a practical approach, focusing on the effective management of risks in the "new era" for businesses operating in China. The ever-evolving larger environment has led to a significant transformation in the nature of risks faced by companies in China over the past decade. Unfortunately, many foreign companies are not adequately prepared to address these emerging risks, which puts them at risk of encountering unforeseen challenges. Since China's declaration of entering a new era in 2017, characterized by consumption-led growth, innovation, territorial integrity, and a proactive role in addressing global challenges, the ramifications of this shift have had an impact on foreign companies operating in the country. Among the various risks that have emerged, three particularly challenging ones are heightened national pride, economic nationalism, and sporadic antiforeign sentiments. As China experiences a surge in national pride and a growing sense of economic nationalism, foreign companies must navigate a more complex and sensitive operating environment. The rise of consumer nationalism, triggered by patriotic sentiments and a desire to support domestic businesses and products, has created unique challenges for foreign brands. Moreover, occasional antiforeign sentiments arising from territorial disputes, historical tensions, or controversies can further complicate the business landscape.

This chapter provides a comprehensive risk management discussion while placing specific emphasis on examining significant instances of consumer nationalism in China over the past five years. It aims to offer practical strategies that could have been implemented by companies to effectively manage such risks. To assess companies' resilience levels, a scale is proposed based on Shimp and Sharma's Consumer Ethnocentrism Tendencies Scale (CETSCALE) and the Consumer Ethnocentrism Extended Scale (CEESCALE). By analyzing major consumer nationalist actions in China, this chapter sheds light on the specific challenges that foreign companies have faced in this evolving landscape. It explores instances where consumer ethnocentrism has influenced consumer behavior and preferences, leading to shifts in brand perception and consumption patterns. Understanding the underlying factors that contribute to consumer nationalism is crucial in formulating effective risk management strategies. Drawing on the insights provided by Shimp and Sharma's CETSCALE and CEESCALE, this chapter proposes a resilience assessment scale. This scale aims to measure companies' ability to navigate and withstand the challenges posed by consumer nationalism. By evaluating factors such as brand perception, consumer loyalty, local adaptation strategies, and crisis management approaches, the scale offers a comprehensive framework for assessing companies' resilience in the face of nationalistic sentiments.

The proposed scale serves as a valuable tool for companies to self-evaluate their preparedness and resilience levels in managing consumer nationalism-related risks in China. By utilizing this scale, companies can identify areas of improvement, develop targeted strategies, and enhance their ability to maintain positive brand perception, consumer loyalty, and business continuity in a changing market environment. Throughout the chapter, practical strategies are discussed, drawing on real-life case studies and best practices. These strategies provide actionable steps that companies can take to proactively manage risks associated with consumer nationalism. From fostering strong relationships with local stakeholders and implementing effective crisis communication plans to adapting products and marketing approaches to align with Chinese cultural values, these strategies aim to enhance companies' resilience and mitigate potential negative impacts.

Overall Risk Overview

On the basis of extensive research and insights from scholars, professionals, and journalists over the past few years (Barry, 2020; Livingston, 2020; McKinsey, 2023), this chapter provides a summary of the overall risks faced by businesses operating in China. These risks are essential for companies to understand and address in order to navigate the complex and evolving business landscape.

Changes in legal and regulatory framework: China's legal and regulatory environment has experienced significant changes in recent years. New laws, regulations, and policies can impact various aspects of business operations, including intellectual property rights, data privacy, market access, and compliance requirements. Keeping up with these alterations and guaranteeing adherence is essential to prevent legal and reputational hazards.

Economic nationalism: Economic nationalism refers to the emphasis on domestic economic interests and the promotion of domestic industries and businesses over foreign competitors. In China, economic nationalism can manifest in various forms, such as preferential treatment for domestic companies, government support for key industries, and policies aimed at reducing reliance on foreign technology. Companies need to navigate this landscape and adapt their strategies to align with local economic priorities.

Heightened national pride and occasional antiforeign sentiments: China's rise as a global power has coincided with a surge in national pride among its citizens. This sense of national pride can occasionally result in antiforeign sentiments, particularly during times of international disputes or controversies. Companies operating in China must be mindful of this sentiment and take proactive measures to address any potential backlash or negative perception.

Higher rates of domestic consumption of goods and services: China's growing middle class and rising disposable incomes have fueled a significant increase in domestic consumption. This presents both opportunities and challenges for companies. While the expanding consumer market offers potential for growth, companies must also adapt their products, marketing strategies, and distribution channels to cater to evolving consumer preferences and demands.

Trade war and other conflicts with the United States: Ongoing trade tensions and conflicts between China and the United States have had far-reaching implications for businesses operating in both countries. Tariffs, trade restrictions, and geopolitical uncertainties can disrupt supply chains, increase costs, and impact market access. Companies need to carefully monitor developments in the China-United States relationship and proactively manage the associated risks.

Case Study

This section will provide a closer examination of three recent consumer nationalism cases that have occurred in China, exploring the triggers that led to these incidents and the consequences that ensued. These cases shed light on the complexities and challenges businesses face when navigating the Chinese market amid nationalist sentiments. By analyzing these cases, we can gain valuable insights into the dynamics of consumer nationalism in China and identify potential strategies for risk management.

Case study 1: Dolce & Gabbana

Trigger

In mid-November 2018, the Italian luxury fashion brand Dolce & Gabbana took to the Chinese social media platform Weibo to launch three brief videos promoting their upcoming Shanghai runway event, named "The Great Show," scheduled for November 21. The videos featured an Asian woman donned in an opulent Dolce & Gabbana dress attempting to eat pizza, spaghetti, and cannoli. Set against the backdrop of Chinese folk music, a Mandarin-speaking voiceover intentionally mispronounced "Welcome to the first episode of 'Eating with Chopsticks' by Dolce & Gabbana," mockingly imitating Chinese speech (Bain, 2018).

The male voice proceeded to mansplain the "proper" way to eat the dishes with chopsticks, mocking the woman for struggling with the oversized cannoli and instructing her to use "small stick-like things" for a pizza margherita in another video. The cannoli video's voiceover remarked, "it can make you feel you are in Italy, but you are in Shanghai".

This advertisement faced severe backlash from Chinese netizens, who deemed it racist, leading to a widespread boycott of the brand. Despite Dolce & Gabbana removing the videos within 24 hours, numerous Chinese celebrities terminated their agreements with the brand. Shortly before the runway show, a fashion blogger shared a screenshot of an alleged chat between designer Stefano Gabbana and an Instagram user, where Gabbana appeared to make derogatory comments about China. This screenshot went viral, sparking the hashtag #boycottdolce. Within hours, many Chinese participants scheduled for the runway withdrew, including D&G's Chinese brand ambassador, Wang Junkai (Bain, 2018).

Gabbana later claimed his Instagram had been hacked, but due to his history of offensive comments, this explanation was met with skepticism. An apology was posted on D&G's official account, alleging both accounts were hacked, expressing respect for China and its people. China's state-run media outlet, Xinhua News Agency, urged foreign brands to respect the Chinese market. Protesters in Italy gathered at Dolce & Gabbana's flagship shop in Milan, while China's e-commerce giants removed D&G products, and retailers like Lane Crawford ceased sales after customer returns (Bain, 2018).

Acknowledging that they "hurt the feelings of the Chinese," expressing love for China and apologizing in Mandarin (Bain, 2018).[1]

Consequence

Following the significant blunder by D&G, several prominent retailers in China have opted to discontinue the brand, including Tmall, JD.com, and Secoo, which play a crucial role for foreign brands seeking to establish

---

[1] Dolce & Gabbana's racism debacle in China could cost it a fortune. https://qz.com/quartzy/1474631/dolce-gabbanas-racism-debacle-in-china-could-cost-it-a-fortune

a presence in the country. Online luxury retailer Yoox Net-a-Porter has removed Dolce & Gabbana from its Chinese-language sites, while Hong Kong-based Lane Crawford has eliminated the brand from both its stores and website. Notably, Chinese celebrities and key opinion leaders (KOLs), influential figures for connecting with Chinese consumers, have distanced themselves from the brand. Many of them were initially slated to attend or participate in the grand Shanghai runway show that the controversial advertisements were originally meant to promote (Bain, 2018).[2]

According to a report by L2, a digital intelligence firm, D&G lost 98 percent of Chinese social media engagement in the first-quarter of 2019 compared to the same period last year. The brand has proven to be an example of how far and fast the mighty can fall in China. Dolce & Gabbana was previously a social media juggernaut, dominating the total share of Weibo engagement among fashion brands in 2018 with a roster of A-list mainland Chinese celebrities including the boy band TFBoys and actress Dilraba Dilmurat. Since the incident, the brand has refrained from signing any major mainland Chinese personalities. For its 2020 Chinese Valentine's Day campaign, it opted for a combination of White and CGI models, referred to as "virtual idols." Although enlisting Chinese celebrity ambassadors and influencers might be a strategy to rebuild trust in the country, Shaun Rein, founder and managing director of China Market Research Group, deems it "career suicide." In June 2021, Hong Kong pop singer Karen Mok faced criticism on social media for featuring D&G apparel in the music video for her new song, "A Woman for All Seasons," indicating that D&G was still grappling to regain favor in China, as reported by BBC. The online backlash has translated into tangible consequences for D&G. In 2018, the brand boasted 58 boutiques in China, according to NPR. However, three years later, its website now lists only 47, with recent closures in Beijing, Shanghai, and Chengdu, as reported by the industry publication *Business of Fashion* (Bain, 2018).

Although D&G's overall revenues from March 2018 to March 2019 grew from 4.9 percent to 1.38 billion euros, its Asia-Pacific market shrank to 22 percent from 25 percent of total turnover. As the *New York Times* reported, the Westerners seemed to had "forgiven" the brand in 2019, but it was still canceled in China. Three years later, it is still eliminated from all major e-tailers in China. As per Bloomberg, D&G's sales in China have experienced a 20 percent recovery compared to the previous year, although they still fall short of pre-incident levels. Despite navigating the social media backlash that

2 Dolce & Gabbana's racism debacle in China could cost it a fortune. https://qz.com/quartzy/1474631/dolce-gabbanas-racism-debacle-in-china-could-cost-it-a-fortune

ensued, the brand successfully retained its existing customer base in China but encountered challenges in attracting new customers, as noted by Dolce.

Case study 2: Marriott

Trigger

On the morning of January 9, 2018, a Weibo user reported that Marriott Hotel Group had classified Tibet, Hong Kong, Macau, and Taiwan as distinct "countries" in its emails and app. The Chinese government regards these cities and territories as integral parts of a unified China and strictly prohibits any expression of sovereignty for these regions. Chinese authorities asserted that Marriott's choice of language violated cybersecurity and advertising laws (Petroff & Jiang, 2018).

From January 9th to January 12th, Marriott issued five consecutive apologies, saying it respected China's sovereignty and territorial integrity as a consistent position and apologized for the corporate misconduct and that it had currently suspended all questionnaires and would conduct a self-examination of the corporate website and its app.

The company mentioned it had rectified a survey sent to members of its loyalty program that incorrectly labeled certain regions, such as Tibet, as countries. Additionally, a comprehensive review of its Chinese website and apps is underway. Marriott is also probing a "careless 'like'" from one of its official social media accounts on a pro-Tibet tweet, which implied support for the position, though Sorenson emphasized that this was untrue. Marriott expressed its intention to take disciplinary action, including potential dismissals, and pledged cooperation with Chinese authorities in their investigation (Petroff & Jiang, 2018).[3]

Consequence

On the evening of January 10, Shanghai Huangpu Police issued a notice stating that on the 9th and 10th they had interviewed the person in charge of the company and that the Huangpu District Market Supervision Bureau had opened a case against it for investigation. The Shanghai Internet Information Office ordered Marriott International to shut down its official Chinese website and Chinese version of its app for one week from 18:00 on the 11th to carry out a comprehensive self-examination and rectification and to thoroughly

---

3 Marriott: China blocks website and app over description of Tibet and Taiwan. https://money.cnn.com/2018/01/11/news/companies/marriott-china-website-app-blocked-tibet-taiwan/index.html

clean up the illegal and non-compliant information. As a result of this incident, many domestic travel platforms started to take down Marriott products, including Meituan and VW Dianping.

On January 12, netizens successively exposed that American Airlines, Zara, Medtronic, and many other companies made similar mistakes, and the Ministry of Civil Aviation and the Municipal Internet Information Office then ordered rectification and requested a public apology.

RevPAR (Revenue per available room) in Greater China

2016.3.31	87.83
2017.6.30	87.22
2017.12.31	92.38
2018.3.31	92.66
2018.6.30	95.94
2018.9.30	93.17
2018.12.31	95.61
2019.9.30	83.66
2020.3.31	29.02

Source: https://www.statista.com/statistics/271129/revpar-marriott-international-inc-hotels-worldwide/

Due to actions Marriott undertook to "correct its mistake" based on the RevPAR in Greater China, it seemed that Marriott was able to bounce back quickly from its listing Taiwan as a country incident. The company's RevPAR continued to rise across the year 2018. Within one week after the shutting down of its official website, the company took multiple actions including public apologies and update its website, which has led to the reopening of its website. Meanwhile, the attention on Marriott also shifted quickly to other brands that were considered as having made the same mistake, which reduced the pressure on Marriot to the same extent.

Case study 3: Versace

Trigger

Late on August 10, 2019, a netizen broke the news on Weibo that Versace T-shirts juxtaposed Hong Kong and Macau with the country, allegedly splitting the country. More than two hours later, at 2:00 am on the 11th, its brand spokesperson Yang Mi first issued a statement saying that she had terminated her contract with Versace, and 10 minutes later, Versace also issued an apology statement on Weibo, saying that the T-shirts involved had all been taken off the shelves and destroyed by July 24th and claiming that Versace loved China and respected its territorial national sovereignty.

In the following day, China's netizens found that many brands including Coach and Givenchy had made the same mistake. The Coach and Givenchy luxury labels, the sports brand Asics, the Calvin Klein clothing line, and the Fresh beauty brand issued apologies on Monday after Chinese netizens launched online campaigns against them for implying that Taiwan and Hong Kong are not part of China on company websites and on T-shirts. Chinese model Liu Wen, serving as Coach's China brand ambassador, declared on Weibo her decision to cease collaboration with Coach. She stated that "the brand has significantly harmed the sentiments of all Chinese and deserves severe criticism" (Campaign, 2019).[4]

The party newspaper, *People's Daily*, said in an editorial on Monday: "Especially during the 'sensitive period' of 'pro-Hong Kong independence activists' creating troubles, this kind of mistake is even more serious."

Consequence

Early in 2019, Michael Kors Holding completed its $2.1 billion acquisition of Versace and renamed itself Capri Holdings. Till now, Capri is still listing Hong Kong with China in its annual reports, while using the phrase Greater China to refer to China, including regions like Hong Kong, Macao, and Taiwan. But Versace had no Chinese spokesman after the backlash.

Case study 4: NBA

Trigger

Daryl Morey, the general manager of the Houston Rockets, posted an image on Twitter expressing support for Hong Kong protests, causing significant controversy due to the heightened emotions surrounding the China-Hong Kong dispute. The tweet sparked outrage, prompting the Rockets organization, including owner Tilman Fertitta, to distance itself from Morey's statement later that night. Subsequently, various Chinese leagues, streaming services, sponsors, and partners severed ties with the Rockets and the NBA. Before the tweet, millions of people in Hong Kong had participated in increasingly violent protests. Initially, the protests revolved around a proposed bill that would have permitted the extradition of Hong Kong residents to China for trial (Mansfield, 2019).

But later protests escalated into violent conflicts damaging the city. However, Morey's tweet used protesters' slogan "Fight for freedom, stand

---

4   Coach, Versace under Chinese fire for problematic country listings | News | Campaign
    Asia.   https://www.campaignasia.com/article/coach-versace-under-chinese-fire-for
    -problematic-country-listings/453617

with Hong Kong." His support for protesters triggered. Swiftly realizing the controversy he had ignited, Morey deleted his tweet within minutes. However, in an era of screenshots and rapid news-sharing, his post was not destined to vanish. On Sunday, having had "a lot of opportunity since that tweet to hear and consider other perspectives," Morey issued a two-part apology on Twitter (Mansfiled, 2019).[5]

However, he claimed to be misunderstood in these two tweets, and Chinese fans saw no explanation of his action or apology, which pushed the backlash further.

The Rockets might devise a creative rationale to terminate Morey, potentially appeasing China and resolving the controversy, which could lead to the restoration of harmony between the organization and China, and on a larger scale, with the NBA. However, The Athletic has reported that such a course of action is unlikely. This approach would contradict the carefully cultivated image of the league and, moreover, punishing or firing Morey would establish a precarious precedent (Mansfield, 2019).[6]

Consequence

Described by the *New York Times* as China's most popular sport, basketball boasts a market with hundreds of millions of fans. According to CNBC, over 640 million people in China tuned in to watch the 2017–2018 NBA season. Chinese-based Tencent, an official broadcasting partner contributing $1.5 billion to the league, suspended all broadcasts involving the Houston Rockets, a move mirrored by China Central Television (CCTV) (Business Insider, 2020).[7] Furthermore, prominent sportswear brands Li-Ning (endorsed by Dwyane Wade and CJ McCollum) and Anta (endorsed by Klay Thompson) announced the termination of their association with the Rockets. Weeks after Morey deleted the tweet, NBA Commissioner Adam Silver admitted substantial losses for the league as tensions escalated. On Saturday, he reiterated this information, confirming its potential impact on salary cap projections for the next season. Even months later, the financial losses continue to be significant. At the 2020 NBA All-Star festivities in Chicago, Commissioner Silver stated that the league has not determined the exact revenue lost due

---

5 A Timeline of the Complicated Controversy Between the NBA and China | Complex.
   https://www.complex.com/sports/2019/10/nba-complicated-history-in-china
6 A Timeline of the Complicated Controversy Between the NBA and China | Complex.
   https://www.complex.com/sports/a/aaron-mansfield/nba-complicated-history-in
   -china
7 Here's why China and the NBA are coming to blows over a tweet | We Are The Mighty.
   https://www.wearethemighty.com/mighty-sports/why-china-nba-over-tweet/

to games being excluded from Chinese state television. Silver mentioned that the NBA could face losses of up to $400 million as Chinese business partners severed ties following social media comments made by Morey. Despite CCTV broadcasting several NBA games due to the league's positive attitude and support during the pandemic, its complete resumption has not occurred to date. In October 2020, Tencent resumed NBA game broadcasts, and the Chinese Foreign Ministry spokesman emphasized the importance of mutual respect in such decisions. However, Chinese netizens seemed unwelcoming of the NBA's return and even criticized Tencent for this move (Young, 2020).[8]

Discussion: Consumer Nationalism Resilience Scale for MNCs

After conducting a comprehensive analysis of the most popular comments on Weibo regarding the 45 selected cases in this study, we have identified five dimensions that significantly influence whether a boycotted product can rebound in sales. These dimensions encompass four subscales each providing a comprehensive framework for understanding the dynamics at play. To develop this scale, I drew upon the foundations laid by Shimp and Sharma's original CETSCALE in 1987. The CETSCALE measures an individual's inclination to favor domestically produced goods over those originating from foreign countries (Nelson and Spence, 1987). Since its inception, Shimp and Sharma's scale has gained significant traction in consumer behavior research, leading to numerous replications and adaptations worldwide. In addition to the CETSCALE, we also incorporated the CEESCALE developed by Siamagka and Balabanis in 2015. This extension to the original scale provides further depth and nuance in assessing consumers' ethnocentric tendencies and their impact on purchasing decisions. By leveraging these established scales and adapting them to the context of boycotted products and sales recovery, we were able to devise a robust measurement tool. The resulting scale encapsulates the various factors that contribute to the potential resurgence of a boycotted product in terms of sales performance. Through our analysis of the most liked comments on Weibo, we identified these dimensions and subscales as key influencers in the bouncing back of boycotted products. By utilizing this scale, researchers and marketers can gain valuable insights into the complex interplay between consumer behavior, ethnocentric tendencies, and the potential recovery of sales for boycotted products.

---

8 NBA will lose hundreds of millions of dollars due to rift with China, commissioner says. https://www.cnbc.com/2020/02/16/nba-will-lose-hundreds-of-millions-of-dollars-due-to-rift-with-china-commissioner-says.html

N°	Item
1	American people should always buy American-made products instead of imports
2	Only those products that are unavailable in US should be imported (*)
3	Buy American-made products. Keep American working
4	American products, first, last, and foremost (*)
5	Purchasing foreign-made products is un-American (*)
6	It is not right to purchase foreign products, because it puts Americans out of jobs (*)
7	A real American should always buy American-made products (*)
8	We should purchase products manufactured in America instead of letting other countries get rich off us (*)
9	It is always best to purchase American products
10	There should be very little trading or purchasing of goods from other countries unless out of necessity
11	Americans should not buy foreign products, because this hurts American business and causes unemployment (*)
12	Curbs should be put on all imports
13	It may cost me in the long run but I prefer to support American products (*)
14	Foreigners should not be allowed to put their products on our markets
15	Foreign products should be taxed heavily to reduce their entry into the US
16	We should buy from foreign countries only those products that we cannot obtain within our own country (*)
17	American consumers who purchase products made in other countries are responsible for putting their fellow Americans out of work (*)

Figure 6.1   Shimp and Sharma's CETSCALE in Consumer Ethnocentrism: Construction and Validation of the CET Scale. *Source*: Shimp and Sharma (1987).

Shimp and Sharma's CETSCALE has established itself as a widely adopted instrument for assessing ethnocentrism in consumer behavior (see Figure 6.1). With its focus on gauging an individual's preference for domestic products over foreign alternatives, the CETSCALE has been extensively employed in research studies spanning various countries and cultures. Its widespread utilization attests to its efficacy in capturing and quantifying consumer ethnocentric tendencies. One of the notable strengths of the CETSCALE lies in its robust construction and reliability. The scale comprises multiple items carefully designed to evaluate the degree of ethnocentrism within individuals. Through systematic validation and rigorous testing, Shimp and Sharma ensured that the scale effectively captures the essence of consumer ethnocentrism. Its reliable measurement properties allow researchers to obtain accurate and consistent data, facilitating meaningful comparisons and generalizations across different contexts. Nevertheless, it is essential to acknowledge the limitations associated with using the CETSCALE. While the scale offers valuable insights into consumer ethnocentrism, its application should be approached with caution.

One important limitation of the CETSCALE is that it solely focuses on measuring attitudes toward domestic and foreign products without considering the specific country of origin. This oversight can lead to potential ambiguities when interpreting the scale's results. For instance, an individual may exhibit a preference for French wine over American wine due to specific quality perceptions or cultural associations, rather than a general inclination toward domestic products. However, since the CETSCALE does not differentiate between countries of origin, it may inaccurately categorize such individuals as ethnocentric. Another noteworthy limitation is the assumption that ethnocentrism can be captured and measured as a unidimensional construct using a single scale. While the CETSCALE has proven valuable in assessing consumer ethnocentrism, some researchers argue that ethnocentrism is better understood as a multidimensional construct. This perspective suggests that multiple aspects, such as cultural distance, perceived threat, and national identity, contribute to ethnocentric behavior and consumer preferences. By considering these various dimensions, researchers can gain a more comprehensive understanding of the complexities underlying consumer ethnocentrism and its impact on behavior.

Recognizing these limitations is crucial for researchers and practitioners working in the field of consumer behavior. Addressing the first limitation could involve incorporating additional variables to capture more nuanced attitudes toward specific countries of origin or products. This approach would provide a more accurate representation of individuals' ethnocentric tendencies and their impact on purchase decisions. To tackle the second limitation, researchers could explore and incorporate multidimensional approaches to measuring ethnocentrism, allowing for a more comprehensive examination of the underlying factors that influence consumer behavior.

Another important limitation of the CETSCALE is its potential cultural bias, which has drawn criticism from researchers. The scale's development was rooted in Western cultural assumptions and perspectives, potentially making it less suitable for non-Western cultures or minority populations within Western countries. Consumer behavior is influenced by diverse cultural contexts, and the CETSCALE may not fully capture the complexities and nuances of consumer ethnocentrism across different cultural backgrounds. When applying the CETSCALE in non-Western cultures, there is a risk of misinterpreting or misrepresenting consumer behavior due to cultural differences that are not adequately accounted for in the scale. Cultural values, norms, and attitudes toward foreign products may vary significantly across different societies, rendering the CETSCALE less applicable or relevant. Therefore, caution should be exercised when using the CETSCALE outside of its original Western cultural context. Despite these limitations, it is important to note that the CETSCALE still retains its value as a useful tool for measuring consumer ethnocentrism, particularly within Western cultures where its development was grounded. It continues to offer valuable insights into consumer preferences for domestic products over foreign alternatives in these contexts. However, researchers should be mindful of the scale's limitations and consider supplementing its use with other measures that capture the specific cultural nuances and contextual factors relevant to the population under study.

Siamagka and Balabanis's CEESCALE, developed in 2015, represents a relatively recent addition to the field of measuring consumer ethnocentrism. This scale distinguishes itself by aiming to capture not only consumers' attitudes toward domestic and foreign products but also their behaviors and intentions regarding them. By encompassing multiple dimensions of consumer ethnocentrism, the CEESCALE provides a comprehensive and insightful tool for researchers and practitioners. One notable strength of the CEESCALE lies in its ability to assess both cognitive and affective components of ethnocentrism. The scale delves beyond mere attitudes and beliefs and also incorporates emotions and behavioral intentions. This multifaceted approach offers a more complete and nuanced understanding of consumer ethnocentric tendencies. By capturing various dimensions of ethnocentrism, such as beliefs, attitudes, emotions, and intentions, the CEESCALE provides a more robust framework for examining and analyzing consumer behavior and preferences.

Furthermore, the CEESCALE's comprehensive nature enables researchers to explore the intricate interplay between different facets of ethnocentrism. By assessing cognitive and affective components, researchers gain insights into the underlying processes that shape consumer behavior. For instance, the scale allows for the examination of how individuals' beliefs and attitudes influence their emotional responses toward domestic and foreign products, which, in turn, impact their intentions and purchasing decisions. This holistic understanding enhances researchers' ability to uncover the complexities of consumer ethnocentrism and its implications. The CEESCALE's incorporation of behavior and intentions expands its practical applicability. By considering not only attitudes but also actual behaviors and intentions, the scale provides a more accurate reflection of consumers' ethnocentric tendencies in real-world contexts. This added dimension offers valuable insights for marketers and policymakers seeking to understand and influence consumer choices and preferences.

In addition to its other strengths, the CEESCALE provides an advantage over the CETSCALE by explicitly accounting for the specific country of origin of the product. This crucial feature addresses a limitation of the CETSCALE, which did not differentiate between different foreign countries. By considering the origin of the product, the CEESCALE enables a more accurate and nuanced measurement of consumer ethnocentrism, particularly in cross-cultural contexts. It acknowledges that consumer preferences and behaviors can vary depending on the specific country of origin, allowing for a more precise understanding of ethnocentric tendencies across different cultural backgrounds. However, it is important to acknowledge that the CEESCALE also has its own limitations. One key limitation is its relatively recent introduction, which means that it has not yet undergone extensive testing and validation in various cultures and contexts. This raises questions about the generalizability of findings derived from the scale and the applicability of the scale in non-Western cultural settings. Given that cultural factors can significantly influence consumer behavior, it is essential to exercise caution when using the CEESCALE outside of its original context and to consider the need for additional validation and adaptation.

To enhance the reliability and validity of the CEESCALE in non-Western cultures, further research is needed to validate its measurement properties across diverse populations. Researchers should conduct studies in different cultural contexts to evaluate the scale's performance, assess its cross-cultural equivalence, and ensure its appropriateness in capturing consumer ethnocentrism across varied cultural backgrounds. By expanding the scope of research, we can gain a better understanding of the scale's strengths and limitations in different contexts, thereby enabling more confident and accurate interpretations of the findings.

Another important limitation of the CEESCALE is its primary focus on consumer behavior toward products, which excludes the assessment of other aspects of ethnocentrism, such as attitudes toward people from different cultures. Ethnocentrism is a multifaceted concept that encompasses not only consumer preferences for domestic or foreign products but also broader attitudes and behaviors related to intercultural interactions. By solely concentrating on product-related behaviors, the CEESCALE may overlook important dimensions of ethnocentrism that influence consumer decisions and interactions with individuals from different cultures. Moreover, similar to the CETSCALE, the CEESCALE assumes that ethnocentrism is a unidimensional construct, treating it as a single scale. However, consumer behavior and attitudes are influenced by various factors, and ethnocentrism is no exception. There is growing recognition among researchers that ethnocentrism is better understood as a multidimensional construct, with multiple factors interacting and shaping consumer behavior. These factors may include cultural distance, perceived threat, national identity, intergroup contact, and others. By adopting a multidimensional approach, researchers can delve deeper into the complexity of ethnocentrism and gain a more comprehensive understanding of its impact on consumer behavior.

Both CETSCALE and CEESCALE are promising tool for measuring consumer ethnocentric tendencies. However, researchers should be aware of its limitations and use it in conjunction with other measures to gain a more comprehensive understanding of consumer behavior. Further research is needed to validate the scale in different cultural contexts and to explore its multidimensional nature. In this research, the structure of both scales are applicable to the nature of the research project, but with a complete opposite angle. This research project aims to find out how resilient are companies when facing nationalistic challenges. In other words, the scale designed will be used by companies instead of consumers.

Both the CETSCALE and CEESCALE demonstrate promise as tools for measuring consumer ethnocentric tendencies. However, it is crucial for researchers to recognize and consider the limitations of these scales and supplement their usage with other measures to obtain a more comprehensive understanding of consumer behavior. Further research is necessary to validate the scales across diverse cultural contexts and explore their multidimensional nature. In the context of a research project aiming to assess the resilience of companies when confronted with nationalistic challenges, the structure of both scales can be applicable, but from a completely different perspective. Rather than assessing consumer attitudes and preferences, the scale designed for this project would be utilized by companies to evaluate their own resilience and adaptability in the face of nationalistic sentiments.

This book aims to delve into how companies navigate and respond to nationalistic pressures. By developing a customized scale, companies can assess their preparedness, strategies, and ability to rebound in the face of consumer boycotts or other nationalistic challenges. The scale would capture relevant dimensions such as company practices, branding, communication strategies, and responses to consumer sentiments related to national identity and domestic versus foreign products. While the CETSCALE and CEESCALE provide insights into consumer ethnocentrism, this book would require adapting the scales to measure the specific resilience and response strategies employed by companies. By using a tailored scale, companies can gain valuable insights into their own performance, make informed decisions, and develop strategies to navigate nationalistic challenges effectively.

Therefore, in light of the book's objective to evaluate the resilience of companies operating in the Chinese market, a customized scale is developed to enable these companies to self-assess their resilience scores. This scale aims to provide a comprehensive framework for companies to evaluate their ability to withstand and adapt to the challenges posed by the Chinese market, with specific weightings assigned to each dimension based on their current importance. The development of this scale involves identifying key dimensions that contribute to a company's resilience in the Chinese market context. These dimensions may include factors such as understanding local consumer preferences, effectively managing local partnerships, navigating regulatory complexities, addressing cultural nuances, building brand reputation, and responding to nationalistic sentiments.

Under each relevant dimensions identified, the scale assigns specific weightings to each dimension based on their current significance and impact in the Chinese market. These weightings reflect the relative importance of each dimension in determining a company's overall resilience score. By assigning weights to the dimensions, the scale acknowledges that not all factors carry equal weight in influencing a company's ability to navigate the Chinese market successfully. Companies can then utilize the developed scale to conduct a self-assessment and evaluate their resilience scores. By considering the weightings assigned to each dimension, companies gain insights into their strengths and weaknesses in relation to key resilience factors in the Chinese market. This self-assessment facilitates a comprehensive evaluation of the company's performance, allowing them to identify areas that require improvement and prioritize their efforts accordingly. Moreover, the customized scale provides a valuable benchmarking tool for companies operating in the Chinese market. By comparing their resilience scores with industry peers or established benchmarks, companies can gain a better understanding of their competitive positioning and identify opportunities for improvement or areas where they excel. It is important to note that the weighting assigned to each dimension may evolve over time, reflecting the dynamic nature of the Chinese market and its shifting demands. Companies should regularly review and update the scale to ensure its relevance and accuracy in capturing the most important factors influencing resilience in the ever-changing market landscape.

1. In the scale developed for companies to self-assess their resilience to operate in the Chinese market, one of the dimensions included is the "Position in China's value chain." This dimension aims to gauge the company's positioning in terms of the value chain hierarchy within the Chinese market. The scale provides multiple options for companies to assess their position, with corresponding weightings assigned based on their potential impact on resilience scores.

Position in China's value chain (30 percent)

Our products are on top of China's value chain.

Our products are at an advanced position of China's value chain.

Our products are in the middle of China's value chain.

Our products are at the bottom of China's value chain.

Priori reasoning: the higher a company's position in China's value chain, the more resilient its operations are likely to be concerning consumer nationalism.

The assigned weightings reflect the prior reasoning that the higher a company's position in China's value chain, the more resilient its operations are likely to be concerning consumer nationalism. This reasoning is based on the assumption that companies with a higher position in the value chain have established a stronger brand reputation, possess advanced technology or expertise, and have a more extensive network of partnerships and relationships in the market. These factors contribute to their ability to navigate challenges related to consumer nationalism more effectively. It is worth noting that the specific weightings for the positions within the value chain would need to be determined based on empirical research or expert consensus to ensure their accuracy and reliability. The weightings may vary depending on the industry, market dynamics, and other contextual factors. Conducting studies or consulting industry experts would provide valuable insights into determining the appropriate weightings for each position within the value chain. By including the "Position in China's value chain" dimension with its respective weightings, the scale enables companies to evaluate their resilience scores in relation to their positioning in the value chain hierarchy. This assessment provides a basis for companies to understand how their position may influence their ability to navigate challenges related to consumer nationalism and make informed decisions on strategies to enhance their resilience in the Chinese market.

2. Another dimension included is "Domestic competition (substitutes)." This dimension aims to evaluate the level of competition faced by the company from domestic substitutes or alternatives within the Chinese market. The scale provides multiple response options for companies to assess the extent of competition, and weightings are assigned based on the expected impact on resilience scores.

Domestic competition (substitutes) (10 percent)

There are no substitutes in China for our products/services at all.

There are very limited substitutes in China for our products/services.

There are quite a few substitutes in China for our products/services.

There are many substitutes in China for our products/services.

Priori reasoning: the less substitutes, the more resilient the company's operations are likely to be with respect to consumer nationalism.

The assigned weightings reflect the prior reasoning that the less competition a company faces from domestic substitutes, the more resilient its operations are likely to be concerning consumer nationalism. This reasoning is based on the assumption that companies with fewer substitutes face less risk of losing market share or facing consumer backlash due to nationalist sentiments. By having fewer alternatives available to consumers, these companies are better positioned to withstand challenges related to consumer nationalism. It is important to note that the specific weightings for the level of domestic competition would need to be determined based on empirical research or expert consensus. Industry-specific factors, market dynamics, and the nature of the products or services should be considered in determining the appropriate weightings. Conducting market analysis, studying competitor landscapes, and seeking expert opinions would provide valuable insights into assigning accurate weightings for each level of domestic competition. By incorporating the "Domestic competition (substitutes)" dimension with its corresponding weightings, the scale allows companies to assess their resilience scores in relation to the level of domestic competition they face. This assessment provides companies with insights into how competition from substitutes may impact their ability to navigate challenges related to consumer nationalism. Armed with this understanding, companies can make informed decisions and implement strategies to enhance their resilience in the face of domestic competition and consumer nationalism in the Chinese market.

3. In the scale developed for companies to self-assess their resilience in the Chinese market, another dimension included is "Domestic employment size." This dimension aims to evaluate the number of domestic employees that a company employs within China. The scale provides multiple response options for companies to indicate their employment size, and weightings are assigned based on the anticipated impact on resilience scores.

Domestic employment size (10 percent)
Our company hires more than 10,000 domestic employees in China.
Our employment size is between 5,000 and 10,000 in China.
Our employment size is between 2,000 and 5,000 in China.
Our employment size is under 2,000 in China.

Priori reasoning: the larger the number of domestic employees, the more resilient the company's operations are likely to be with respect to consumer nationalism.

The assigned weightings reflect the priori reasoning that the larger the number of domestic employees a company has, the more resilient its operations are likely to be concerning consumer nationalism. This reasoning is based on the assumption that companies with a significant domestic workforce have a stronger connection to the local community and can potentially mitigate the impact of consumer nationalism through their contribution to employment opportunities and economic growth. Moreover, a larger domestic employment size may enhance the company's ability to navigate local regulations and engage in proactive stakeholder management. By including the "Domestic employment size" dimension with its respective weightings, the scale enables companies to assess their resilience scores based on the number of domestic employees they have in China. This assessment provides companies with insights into how their employment size may influence their ability to navigate challenges related to consumer nationalism. Companies can then strategize and prioritize efforts to enhance their resilience in the Chinese market by leveraging their domestic employment size and its potential positive impact on stakeholder perceptions.

4. Political conflicts (values in tension) with the company's home country (40 percent)

   Our home country has unsolvable conflicts with China.
   Our home country has constant disputes with China.
   Our home country has occasional disputes with China.
   Our home country has no disputes with China.

This dimension assesses the level of political conflicts or disputes between the company's home country and China. The higher the intensity of conflicts, the lower the resilience score, as it indicates potential challenges and risks in operating in the Chinese market.

Priori reasoning: the less conflicts China has with the company's home country, the more resilient the company's operations are likely to be with respect to consumer nationalism.

5. The last dimension included is "Customer loyalty." This dimension aims to evaluate the level of loyalty exhibited by the company's customers toward its products or services. The scale provides multiple response options for companies to assess customer loyalty, and weightings are assigned based on the expected impact on resilience scores.

   Customer loyalty (10 percent)
   Your customers are attached to your products/services.

Your customers are saying positive things about your products/services.
Your customers are recommending your products/services to others.
Your customers consider your products/services first choices in purchase decision-making.

Priori reasoning: the higher a company's customer loyalty level is in China, the more resilient its operations are likely to be concerning consumer nationalism.

By incorporating the "Customer loyalty" dimension with its corresponding weightings, the scale allows companies to assess their resilience scores based on the loyalty exhibited by their customers. This assessment provides companies with insights into how customer loyalty may influence their ability to navigate challenges related to consumer nationalism. Armed with this understanding, companies can implement strategies to enhance customer loyalty and thereby bolster their resilience in the Chinese market, considering the potential impact of consumer nationalism on customer behavior.

In addition to the self-assessment tool, this chapter also provides some practical strategic communication strategies that foreign companies can consider in dealing with consumer nationalism in China, including adapting marketing messages to local cultural values; emphasizing local presence and contributions; strengthening corporate social responsibility (CSR) initiatives; enhancing transparency and communication; engaging with KOLs and influencers; establishing partnerships with local brands; adapting to Chinese social media platforms; and continuously monitoring and addressing consumer sentiment.

Tailor marketing and advertising campaigns to align with Chinese cultural values and preferences are particularly important in the current context. This includes incorporating local traditions, customs, and symbols that resonate with the target audience. By demonstrating an understanding and respect for Chinese culture, companies can foster a stronger connection with consumers.

Companies could also demonstrate commitment to the local market by showcasing their investments, job creation, and contributions to the local economy. This can help alleviate concerns related to foreign influence and demonstrate the company's dedication to supporting China's development.

Companies could also engage in CSR activities that address social and environmental concerns within China. By actively contributing to local communities and addressing pressing issues, companies can build goodwill, enhance their reputation, and mitigate negative perceptions associated with consumer nationalism.

It is also important to foster open and transparent communication with Chinese consumers. This involves actively addressing concerns, responding to feedback, and providing clear information about the company's operations, sourcing practices, and commitment to quality. Building trust through transparent communication can help alleviate doubts and counteract negative sentiment. Companies might collaborate with influential individuals and content creators in China to promote positive narratives about the company and its products/services. Leveraging the power of KOLs and influencers can help shape public perception, generate positive word-of-mouth, and counteract negative sentiment.

Collaborating with local brands or establishing joint ventures to demonstrate a commitment to local partnerships and to create mutually beneficial opportunities is another option. This can help build trust, establish credibility, and align the company with local interests. Leveraging popular Chinese social media platforms such as WeChat, Weibo, and Douyin (TikTok) to engage with Chinese consumers directly. Create engaging content, share relevant information, and actively participate in conversations to foster a positive brand image and strengthen consumer connections.

Companies should also stay vigilant and monitor consumer sentiment and feedback through social listening and market research. Actively address concerns, respond to criticisms, and adapt strategies based on consumer insights to maintain a positive brand perception.

Implementing these strategic communication strategies can help foreign companies navigate consumer nationalism in China by fostering trust, demonstrating cultural sensitivity, and building strong connections with Chinese consumers. It is important for companies to tailor these strategies to their specific circumstances, continuously evaluate their effectiveness, and remain adaptable in the ever-evolving Chinese market.

Chapter 7

CONCLUSION

The COVID-19 pandemic has left a significant and lasting impact on the Chinese consumer market and real-estate sector. While initial recovery efforts began in late 2020, the revival of consumer spending has been slower than expected due to persistent concerns about the virus and economic uncertainty. As a result, Chinese consumers have become more cautious in their spending habits, with a shift toward health-related products, e-commerce, and digital services. This shift has affected various industries and has been particularly challenging for small and medium-sized enterprises.

In the real-estate sector, the pandemic led to a severe downturn, with declining property sales and investments. Government regulations aimed at curbing property speculation and controlling housing prices have further complicated the situation, making it difficult for developers to recover. Overseas corporations operating in China, especially those in the real-estate and construction sectors, have also faced challenges, with declining property values, increased regulatory scrutiny, and a slower economic recovery affecting profitability and expansion plans. The road to recovery for both the consumer market and the real-estate sector in China appears to be long and challenging, requiring adaptation and strategic planning to navigate the evolving economic landscape.

This chapter delves into the profound implications of the book's discussion by placing it within the broader context of current events. In recent years, the world has witnessed a noticeable surge in nationalism, a trend that has been further accelerated by the advent of the COVID-19 pandemic. Governments have resorted to actions such as imposing border shutdowns, engaging in fierce competition for essential medical supplies, and engaging in blame games, attributing the origins of the disease to one another. These actions have collectively propelled the wave of nationalism to new heights on a global scale. As a consequence, we find ourselves amid renewed geopolitical uncertainty and pervasive social unrest that show no signs of abating. The continuous presence of these challenges poses a considerable dilemma for policymakers and business operators alike, as they strive to navigate an increasingly complex landscape.

The chapter undertakes a comprehensive examination of these challenges, shedding light on their multifaceted nature. It particularly emphasizes the rise of nationalism and the interference of governments in markets, both of which pose significant threats to the stability of the global economic system. By analyzing the interplay between these factors, the chapter provides a critical understanding of the risks and obstacles faced by policymakers and business operators in today's interconnected world.

Existing Threats to the Global Economic System

According to the World Bank's latest Global Economic Prospects report, the global economy, after experiencing a robust rebound in 2021, is now on the brink of a significant deceleration. This slowdown is primarily attributed to the emergence of new threats posed by COVID-19 variants, as well as a simultaneous increase in inflation, debt levels, and income inequality. These combined factors pose a substantial risk to the ongoing recovery efforts in emerging and developing economies. The world finds itself at a critical juncture, where the convergence of multiple challenges has the potential to impede economic progress on a global scale. The persistence of COVID-19 variants has resulted in renewed disruptions and uncertainties, casting a shadow over the recovery process. The threat of new waves of infections and the necessity for precautionary measures, such as lockdowns and travel restrictions, are creating headwinds that hamper economic activity and dampen consumer and investor confidence.

Additionally, the World Bank's report highlights the concerning rise in inflation, which further exacerbates the economic outlook. Elevated inflation rates increase production costs, erode purchasing power, and impose a burden on households and businesses alike. Furthermore, mounting levels of debt and widening income inequality pose significant challenges to achieving sustainable and inclusive growth. The burden of debt servicing can stifle investment and limit the capacity of governments to implement effective stimulus measures. Meanwhile, rising income inequality undermines social cohesion and may hinder the ability of individuals and communities to fully participate in and contribute to economic development. As the global economy faces this slowdown, there is a worrisome divergence in growth rates between advanced economies and emerging and developing economies. Advanced economies, equipped with greater access to vaccines and fiscal resources, are expected to experience a more rapid recovery. However, emerging and developing economies, constrained by various structural and systemic challenges, are at greater risk of falling behind, exacerbating existing disparities.

Since Russia's invasion of Ukraine, global geopolitical risks have surged, creating a tumultuous landscape for the global economy. The World Economic Forum's Global Risks Report 2023 explicitly highlights the disruption caused by the outbreak of war in Ukraine, shattering the nascent "new normal" that was beginning to take shape after the COVID-19 pandemic. The report underscores how this conflict has triggered a fresh series of crises in crucial areas such as food and energy, unraveling decades of progress that had aimed to address these very challenges. The repercussions of the war in Ukraine are expected to reverberate throughout the global economy, leading to a myriad of concerns. Investors, market participants, and policymakers are bracing themselves for an economic drag, inflationary pressures, heightened uncertainty, and an increased risk of severe adverse outcomes. These projections align with the insights provided by Caldara et al. (2022), who assert that the war is likely to have a dampening effect on the global economy while simultaneously fueling inflation. The escalation of geopolitical tensions introduces a heightened level of uncertainty that can hinder business and consumer confidence, potentially leading to a slowdown in investment and economic activity.

Research conducted by Ozili (2022), utilizing global data along with specific data from the Euro Area, Ukraine, and Russia, further supports these concerns. The findings indicate an increase in the global Purchasing Managers' Index, reflecting a decline in business sentiment and activity, while also revealing a surge in the world price of food and food ingredients. The sanctions imposed on Russia, although intended to exert pressure on the country, have had unintended spillover effects on the global economy, primarily manifesting as disruptions in the global supply chain. These disruptions have disrupted trade flows, leading to supply shortages and higher prices for essential goods, ultimately impacting economies worldwide. The consequences of Russia's invasion of Ukraine and the subsequent international response are anticipated to deal a substantial blow to global economic prospects. The OECD (2022) concurs with this assessment, emphasizing the setback that these events pose to the trajectory of the global economy. The heightened geopolitical tensions and the resulting economic consequences further underscore the imperative for international cooperation, dialogue, and diplomatic efforts to de-escalate the conflict and seek peaceful resolutions.

Therefore, the invasion of Ukraine by Russia in February 2022 and the subsequent international response have triggered a series of negative consequences for global economic prospects.

Ozili (2022) highlights the anticipated drag on the global economy, inflationary pressures, disruptions in supply chains, and increased uncertainty. These developments pose significant challenges for investors, market participants, and policymakers alike, underscoring the urgent need for concerted efforts to address and resolve the geopolitical tensions in order to safeguard global economic stability and progress. Addressing these multifaceted challenges necessitates a coordinated and comprehensive response from governments, international institutions, and other stakeholders. It is crucial to prioritize efforts that mitigate the impact of COVID-19 variants, including effective vaccination campaigns, robust healthcare systems, and coordinated international cooperation. Moreover, policies that tackle inflationary pressures, promote sustainable debt management, and foster inclusive growth must be implemented to ensure a more equitable and resilient recovery for all economies.

In summary, the global economy's path toward recovery has encountered formidable obstacles, including the threat of COVID-19 variants, rising inflation, mounting debt levels, and widening income inequality. The World Bank's report emphasizes the urgent need for proactive measures to mitigate these risks and foster a more balanced and sustainable trajectory. By addressing these challenges head-on, the international community can strive toward a future where economic prosperity is shared and resilient across all nations.

The Rise of Nationalism in the World

In recent years, there has been an undeniable surge in populist movements and waves of nationalism that have reverberated across the globe (Quirk, 2022). These phenomena have captured the attention of scholars, policymakers, and the public alike, as they reshape political landscapes and challenge established norms. Understanding the roots of nationalism is crucial in comprehending the factors that contribute to its rise. Nationalism often emerges as a response to the forces of globalization. Delanty (2006) and Bonikowski (2016) argue that the rise of nationalism can be seen as a defensive reaction against the perceived erosion of national identities and cultural homogeneity brought about by increasing global interconnectedness. As societies become more interconnected, individuals may feel a sense of insecurity or displacement, which can fuel the rise of nationalist sentiments. In this context, nationalism acts as a protective shield for national values, traditions, and identities in the face of perceived threats from globalizing forces.

Furthermore, scholars such as Greenfeld (2006; 2012) suggest that nationalism is influenced by industrialization, globalization, and capitalism. These processes often lead to significant social and economic transformations within societies. As traditional social structures undergo upheaval and economic disparities widen, nationalism can arise as a response to these changes. It becomes a way for individuals to assert their identity and interests, particularly against perceived external threats or perceived injustices resulting from globalization and capitalism. The complex relationship between nationalism and globalization is characterized by a tension between the forces of integration and those of differentiation. While globalization can foster interconnectedness, it can also generate anxieties related to cultural assimilation, economic inequality, and loss of national sovereignty. These tensions can fuel the rise of nationalist movements, as individuals seek to protect what they perceive as their national heritage, values, and interests.

As the global political landscape undergoes a shift toward more insular state-centric perspectives, there is a notable contraction in how individuals perceive their place and connection to the world. This retrenchment is characterized by a narrowing of worldviews and a reevaluation of one's relational identity within a global context. Benedict Anderson, in his influential work "Imagined Communities," contends that the nation is an imagined political community. In an era of increasing globalization, the concept of the nation has faced challenges as borders have become more porous and the world seemingly more interconnected. The forces of globalization have fostered a sense of a borderless world, blurring the traditional boundaries that define nations and reshaping perceptions of identity and belonging. However, the COVID-19 pandemic has paradoxically witnessed a strengthening of the nation-state. In response to the public health crisis, governments worldwide have taken extraordinary measures, such as imposing travel bans and border closures, in an attempt to mitigate the spread of the virus. These actions have reasserted the significance of national borders and sovereignty, reinforcing the notion of the nation-state as a primary political entity responsible for safeguarding the well-being of its citizens.

The pandemic has highlighted the tension between the forces of globalization and the resilience of national identities and institutions. While global interconnectedness remains a defining feature of the contemporary world, the pandemic has demonstrated the enduring relevance and power of the nation-state as a locus of governance and decision-making. The actions taken during this crisis have reaffirmed the significance of national borders as a means to protect public health and security, albeit at the cost of limiting cross-border mobility and international cooperation. This retrenchment of the nation-state amid the pandemic reflects a broader trend of shifting global political dynamics. The rise of nationalist movements and the resurgence of protectionist policies in recent years indicate a growing emphasis on state sovereignty and a reassertion of national interests. This shift in perspectives challenges the idea of a borderless world, prompting individuals to reconsider their place within the global community and reevaluate the importance of national identity.

Consequently, this exclusionary mindset is reshaping the public's "imagination" of who belongs to the "imagined community." With this mindset, one's national identity is prioritized over all other elements including cultural roots, family ties, and so on. It heats up nationalism because nationalism is easily ignited in circumstances like this. Therefore, we have seen the rise of bias against some groups, the rise of fear, and what's also emerged is a narrower way of looking at bilateral relations with certain countries, where similarities and shared interests have not been paid enough attention.

What's been emphasized by these actions is the exclusivity of nationality and reinforcement of the notion that closed borders protect us from outside dangers. As Singh (2022) argues in her article titled "How Exclusionary Nationalism Has Made the World Socially Sicker from COVID-19," the brand of exclusive nationalism has heightened the danger of the COVID-19 pandemic for our political framework more than it would have been otherwise. The world was already suffering from a lot of problems prior to COVID-19, including issues in the United States, Russia, China, India, and more. Minorities and immigrants have been targeted by dominant ethnic groups in some countries. Derived from our innate inclination to link foreigners with disease, every epidemic possesses the capacity to heighten divisions between ingroups and outgroups, often leading to scapegoating of the latter. However, this detrimental tendency embedded in all contagions has particularly thrived during the COVID-19 pandemic. This phenomenon finds fertile ground in the soil of exclusionary nationalism, where boundaries between countries and within countries, such as those between majority and minority groups, were already deeply entrenched.

In addition to the aforementioned observations, it is crucial to highlight the escalating impact of the COVID-19 pandemic on the global economic landscape. The outbreak of the pandemic has disrupted economies worldwide, leading to unprecedented challenges and prompting countries to reevaluate their priorities. As nations grappled with the consequences of the health crisis, there has been a noticeable erosion of confidence in supranational forms of governance and a resurgence of protectionist and nationalist tendencies. The COVID-19 pandemic has exposed vulnerabilities in global supply chains and highlighted the dependence of many countries on external sources for essential goods and services. This realization has spurred a reevaluation of economic strategies, with a growing emphasis on self-reliance and national interests. Governments are now prioritizing domestic industries and focusing on building resilient economies that can withstand future shocks.

The United States and the United Kingdom, in particular, have experienced a significant shift toward economic nationalism, which is surprising given the trajectory of these nations in previous years (Rammal et al., 2022). Both countries have witnessed a resurgence of nationalist sentiment, characterized by policies aimed at protecting domestic industries, renegotiating trade agreements, and reducing reliance on international markets. This shift marks a departure from the prevailing trend of globalization and international cooperation that had been prominent for decades. The implications of this growing wave of economic nationalism are far-reaching. It threatens the progress made through various global trading arrangements, as barriers to trade are erected and cooperation between nations is strained. The internationalization of services, which has been a driving force for economic growth and prosperity, faces new challenges as countries prioritize their own interests over global collaboration.

The study conducted by Burgoon (2013) sheds light on an important aspect of the relationship between national welfare compensation and the backlash against globalization, foreign firms, and immigration. By analyzing national elections in OECD member countries over a span of more than four decades, Burgoon identifies a noteworthy trend: the intensity of the backlash is higher when national welfare compensation is moderate, but it decreases when welfare compensation reaches higher levels. This finding suggests that the level of welfare compensation plays a significant role in shaping public sentiment toward globalization, foreign firms, and immigration. When welfare compensation is moderate, there appears to be a heightened sense of insecurity and dissatisfaction among citizens, which can manifest as a backlash against these aspects of globalization. This backlash is characterized by a rise in nationalism, a revival of economic nationalism, and an anti-globalization sentiment. The link between these phenomena and international trade, capital openness, and immigration flows becomes evident when considering the interconnectedness of these factors. Globalization, through increased international trade and capital flows, has facilitated the movement of goods, services, and capital across borders. While this has brought about numerous economic benefits, it has also created challenges and disruptions in local labor markets and industries. These disruptions, combined with concerns about the impact of immigration on employment and social cohesion, can contribute to the rise of nationalism and anti-globalization sentiment. In summary, we are currently witnessing a growth in this stance, especially in countries where this would scarcely have been predicted a few years ago (Globerman, 2017).

The COVID-19 pandemic has additionally eroded supranational modes of governance and fueled the inclination toward protectionism and economic nationalism (Davies, 2020).

Open Conclusion

In addition to the points already mentioned, this book emphasizes the growing risk of nationalist consumer outrage for businesses operating in China or dealing with Chinese markets. As China faces mounting diplomatic challenges abroad, multinational companies must exercise extreme caution when navigating the intricacies of the world's second-largest economy. This chapter aims to provide a broader perspective on the discussion by highlighting the global rise of nationalism in recent years, which has been further accelerated by the COVID-19 pandemic. The rise of nationalism is a trend that extends beyond China, encompassing countries around the world. People's identification with their nation and its values has gained prominence, shaping consumer behavior and attitudes toward foreign entities. This global context of rising nationalism sets the stage for understanding the specific challenges faced by foreign brands operating in China.

In the forthcoming years, uncertainty emerges as a key theme, driven by significant shifts in the nature of the relationship between the United States and China, as well as widespread unsettlement in the global landscape. These geopolitical dynamics create an environment where foreign brands operating in China face increasing risks and complexities. Navigating this landscape requires a keen understanding of the evolving dynamics between nations and the ability to adapt strategies accordingly. This book aims to provide practical strategies for foreign brands to engage in more effective strategic communication and public relationship management in China. Recognizing the importance of understanding the local market and cultural nuances, the book offers insights and recommendations to help businesses navigate the challenges posed by nationalist sentiment and evolving geopolitical landscapes. Effective strategic communication and public relationship management can be instrumental in building trust, mitigating potential backlash, and maintaining positive brand perception in the Chinese market. By tailoring their approaches to the unique dynamics of China's nationalist sentiment, foreign brands can enhance their ability to engage with consumers, manage crises, and foster positive relationships with stakeholders.

In conclusion, this book emphasizes the increasing risk of nationalist consumer outrage for businesses operating in China or dealing with Chinese markets. It places this discussion within the broader context of the global rise of nationalism, with the COVID-19 pandemic acting as a catalyst. The evolving relationship between the United States and China, combined with broader uncertainties in the world, introduces additional challenges for foreign brands in China. Through practical strategies for strategic communication and public relationship management, this book seeks to provide valuable guidance for navigating these complexities and building successful brand presence in China's dynamic market.

APPENDIX

Brand name	Trigger	Consequences
Marc Jacobs	Supporting the Free Tibet Movement (2014, 2016, 2018)	Minor, still in Chinese market and returned to profitability in 2020
KFC	South China Sea Dispute (2016)	Minor, small protests
Virgin	Racism (2016)	Minor, Virgin investigated and clarified
Anastasia	Tibet, attended a meeting with Dalai and praised him online (2016)	Minor, apologized and deleted related content
Lush	Tibet (2016)	Minor, as Lush only sells its products in Hong Kong
Lancome (L'Oreal Group)	Hong Kong (2016)	Minor, apologized and claimed that He Yunshi was not its Spokesperson, market capitalization dropped by 18 billion in three days, but recovered soon
Listerine	Hong Kong (2016)	Minor, still popular online and strongly recommended
DHC	Support for Japanese right-wing organizations (2017)	Minor, small protests, still recommended by celebrities
Spreadshirt	Racism, "save a dog, eat a Chinese" (2017)	Hard to assess, not in China's market, apologized and claimed that it was the designer's fault
Pola	Discrimination of Chinese consumers (2017)	Minor, apologized for the shop owner's individual behavior and closed the particular shop
Tarte	Racism, "ching chong" (2017)	Minor, apologized and claimed that it was the mistake of an internal member
Lotte Mart	Helped THAAD deployment in Republic of Korea (2017)	Significant, withdrew from the Chinese market in 2018, 99 shops all closed
Smashbox (Estee Lauder)	Claimed to refuse to sell products in China	Minor, can be bought online but not very popular

(*Continued*)

(Continued)

Brand name	Trigger	Consequences
APA Hotel	Right-wing books denying Nanjing Massacre (2017)	Significant, banned by National Tourism Administration
Marriott Hotel	Hong Kong, Tibet, Macao, Taiwan (2018)	Relatively significant but recovered now, apologized for five times and was ordered to shut down its website for a week
Estee Lauder	Alleged mistreatment of Chinese consumer (2017), Hong Kong, Taiwan (2019)	Minor, still endorsed by celebrities and sales in Asian-Pacific area reached 7.29 billion in 2019
D&G	Discrimination (2018)	Significant, lost 98% market
Balenciaga	Mistreatment of Chinese shoppers (2018)	Apologized twice, recovered in months
YG Entertainment	Incomplete map and discrimination (2018)	Minor, apologized and deleted related content, singers had minor impact
Benz	Tibet, advertisement using the saying of Dalai (2018)	Minor, apologized and deleted the advertisement, sold 6.7 billion cars in 2018, grew rapidly
NBA	Hong Kong (2019)	Significant, still banned by state media
The Body Shop	Supporting International Tibet Support Network (2018, 2009)	Minor, small protests, sales grew by 17% in 2018
Philipp Plein	Shirts with clown image of the Qing dynasty and "F-UC-K YOU CHINA" (2018, 2007)	Minor, claimed that it was an innovation, still popular on social media
Versace	Hong Kong, Macao (2019)	Minor, apologized, took related products off shelves and destroyed
Coach	Hong Kong, Taiwan (2019)	Minor, apologized and took related products off shelves
Asics	Hong Kong, Taiwan (2019)	Minor, sales in the Greater China area dropped by 0.6%
Givenchy	Hong Kong, Taiwan (2019)	Minor, apologized and had new spokespersons in 2020
Clarins	Hong Kong, Taiwan (2019)	Minor, still strongly recommended on Chinese social media (more than 20,000 notes on Xiaohongshu)
Cle De Peau	Hong Kong, Taiwan (2019)	Minor, still strongly recommended by celebrities like LiJiaqi (more than 270,000 notes on Xiaohongshu)
Swarovski	Hong Kong (2019)	Minor, changed its spokesperson in 2021 to TangYan (more than 180,000 notes on Xiaohongshu)

(Continued)

(Continued)

Brand name	Trigger	Consequences
Fresh	Kong Kong (2019)	Minor, small protests
Jaeger-LeCoultre	Hong Kong, Taiwan (2019)	Minor, still strongly recommended on Chinese social media (more than 20,000 notes on Xiaohongshu)
NBA	Hong Kong (2019)	Significant, still banned by CCTV
Nike	Xinjiang (2021)	Minor, wearable tech fills a gap in China's value chain, ahead of Olympics
H&M	Xinjiang (2021)	Erased from the Internet, outlets shuttered in several cities
Calvin Klein	Xinjiang (2021)	Lost brand ambassador partnerships
Zara	Xinjiang (2021)	Minor, its parent company Inditex removed the statement against cotton from Xinjiang, revenues grew by 56% in the second quarter compared to the same period in 2020
Uniqlo	Xinjiang (2021)	Significant, sales in April on Tmall dropped by 20%
Muji	Xinjiang (2021)	Significant, its share price fell by 7% on April 15th, claimed to continue to use cotton from Xinjiang
Adidas	Xinjiang (2021)	Significant, sales in the Asian-Pacific area dropped by 15.9% in the second quarter in 2021, sales in April on Tmall dropped by 78%
Puma	Xinjiang (2021)	Minor, sales in the second quarter of 2021 doubled compared to 2020
New Balance	Xinjiang (2021)	Minor, small protests
Burberry	Xinjiang (2021)	Minor, cooperation with Honor of King ended, but sales in China grew by 30% in the first half year of 2021 compared to the same period of 2020
Converse	Xinjiang (2021)	Minor, small protests
Tommy Hilfiger (PVH Corp)	Xinjiang (2021)	Minor, revenues grew by 41% in the second quarter compared to the same period in 2020

Source: Author's own compilation.

BIBLIOGRAPHY

Abdelal, R. (2001) *National Purpose in the World Economy: Post-Soviet States in Comparative Perspective*, xi, 221. Ithaca: Cornell University Press.

Acheson, F. (2021) "Market sights – Greater China." https://www.nzte.govt.nz/blog/market-insights-greater-china-3. Viewed 20 June 2022.

Agbonifoh, B. and J. U. Elimimian (1999) "Attitudes of Developing Counties Towards 'Country-of-Origin' Products in an Era of Multiple Brands." *Journal of International Consumer Marketing* 11: 97–116.

Altintas, M. H. and T. Tokol (2007) "Cultural Openness and Consumer Ethnocentrism: An Empirical Analysis of Turkish Consumers." *Journal of Marketing Intelligence & Planning* 25(4): 308–25.

Anderson, B. (1991) *Imagined Communities: Reflections on the Origin and Spread of Nationalism*. London: Verso.

Anholt, S. (1998) "Nation-brands of the Twenty-first Century." *Journal of Brand Management* 5(6): 395–406.

Anholt, S. (2006) *Competitive Identity: The New Brand Management for Nations, Cities and Regions*. Basingstoke: Palgrave Macmillan.

"Anti-Carrefour Protests Hit China." France 24, 1 May 2008, https://www.france24.com/en/20080501-anti-carrefour-protests-hit-china-china-carrefour. Accessed 5 April 2023.

Ashenfelter, O., S. Ciccarella, and J. S. Howard (2007) "French Wine and the U.S. Boycott of 2003: Does Politics Really Affect Commerce?" *Journal of Wine Economics* 2(1): 55–74.

Bahaee, M. and M. J. Pisani (2009) "Are Iranian Consumers Poised to Buy American in a Hostile Bilateral Environment?" *Business Horizons* 52(3): 223–32.

Balabanis, G. and A. Diamantopoulos (2004) "Domestic Country Bias, Country of Origin Effects, and Consumer Ethnocentrism: A Multidimensional Unfolding Approach." *Journal of the Academy of Marketing Science* 32(1): 80–95.

Barry, D. (2020) "Managing Risk in the 'New Era'." *Chinese Business Review*. https://www.chinabusinessreview.com/managing-risk-in-the-new-era/.

Becic, M. (2017) "An Assessment of Consumer Ethnocentrism Tendencies Scale among University Students: The Case of Turkish and Bosnian Student Inquiry." *Sarajevo Journal of Society Sciences* 2(1): 119–30.

Bergsten, C., C. Freeman, N. Lardy, and D. Mitchell (2009) *China's Rise: Challenges and Opportunities*. Peterson Institute for International Economics.

Billig, M. (1995) *Banal Nationalism*, London, Thousand Oaks, New York: Sage.

Blanchard, B. (2008) "Chinese Protesters Target Carrefour Again." *Reuters*, 1 May, https://www.reuters.com/article/us-china-carrefour-idUSSP252272008050. Accessed 19 May 2023.

Boieji, J., S. T. U. Tuah, A. Alwie, and A. Maisarah (2010) "Local vs Foreign Made: Are Malaysians Ethnocentric?" *The IUP Journal of Marketing Management* 4(3): 6–23.

Bonikowski, B. (2016) "Nationalism in Settled Times." *Annual Review of Sociology* 42(1): 427–49.

Brass, P. R. (1991) *Ethnicity and Nationalism: Theory and Comparison*. Newbury Park, CA: Sage.

Breslin, s. (2005) "Power and Production: Rethinking China's Global Economic Role." *Review of International Studies* 31(4): 735–53, https://doi.org/10.1017/s026021050500673x.

Breuilly, J. (1993) *Nationalism and the State*, 2nd edition. Manchester: Manchester University Press.

Bruun, O. (1991) *Business and Bureaucracy in a Chinese City: An Ethnography of Private Business Households in Contemporary China*. Berkeley: Institute of East Asian Studies.

Burgoon, B. (2013) "Inequality and Anti-globalization Backlash by Political Parties." *European Union Politics* 14(3): 408–35.

Buzan, B. and G. Segal (1994) "Rethinking East Asian Security." *Survival* 36(2): 3–21.

Cabestan, J.-P. (2005) "The Many Facets of Chinese Nationalism." *China Perspectives*, https://journals.openedition.org/chinaperspectives/2793#citedby.

Caldara, D., S. Conlisk, M. Locaviello, and M. Penn (2022) "The Effect of the War in Ukraine on Global Activity and Inflation." *Economic Research*, 27 May, https://www.federalreserve.gov/econres/notes/feds-notes/the-effect-of-the-war-in-ukraine-on-global-activity-and-inflation-20220527.html.

Castello, E. and S. Mihelj (2018) "Selling and Consuming the Nation: Understanding Consumer Nationalism." *Journal of Consumer Culture* 18(4) 558–576.

Chao, L. and R. H. Myers (1998) "China's Consumer Revolution: The 1990s and Beyond." *Journal of Contemporary China* 7(18): 351–68.

Chen, S. M. (1996) "Min zu zhu yi: Fu xing zhi dao? [Nationalism: A Way for Revival?]." *DF* 2, 74–6.

Chen, X. (2020) "Nationalism, Patriotism, and the Role of Social Media in China." *International Journal of Marketing Studies* 12(2): 90–98.

China Economy Website (Zhongguo Jingji Wang). (2009) "2001: APEC — 'Zhongguo nian' de lishi huazhang [2001: APEC — The historical section of 'Year of China']." http://views.ce.cn/fun/corpus/ce/7/200902/06/t20090206_18138037.shtml.

"Chinese Communist Party Targets Private Sector." Center for Strategic and International Studies, 6 July 2020, https://www.csis.org/analysis/chinese-communist-party-targets-private-sector.

Christensen, T. (1996). "Chinese Realpolitik." *Foreign Affairs* 75(5): 37–40.

"Coach, Versace under Chinese Fire for Problematic Country Listings." Campaign Asia, 5 December 2018, https://www.campaignasia.com/article/coach-versace-under-chinese-fire-for-problematic-country-listings/453617.

Crane, G. T. (1998) "Economic Nationalism: Bringing the Nation Back." *Millennium: Journal of International Studies* 27(1): 55–75.

Credit Suisse. (2018) "Emerging Consumer Survey." https://www.credit-suisse.com/media/assets/corporate/docs/about-us/research/publications/ecs-2018.pdf.

Credit Swiss. (2018) "Emerging Consumer Survey 2018." https://www.credit-suisse.com/about-us/en/reports-research/csri.html. Viewed 20 January 2023.

Cuadras, X. and J. M. Raya (2016) "Boycott or *Buycott*? Internal Politics and Consumer Choices." *The B.E. Journal of Economic Analysis and Policy* 16(1): 185–218.

Darian-Smith, E. (2020) "Globalizing Education in Times of Hyper-Nationalism, Rising Authoritarianism, and Shrinking Worldviews." *New Global Studies* 14(1): 47.

Davies, S. (2020) "Pandemics and the Consequences of COVID-19." *Economic Affairs* 40: 131–37.

"Davos'23: The Global Economy Is Under Pressure, but How Bad Is It? Two Experts Share Insights." *World Economic Forum*, 17 January 2023, https://www.weforum.org /agenda/2023/01/davos23-the-global-economy-is-under-pressure-but-how-bad-is-it -two-experts-share-insights/.

Dean, M. (1991) *The Constitution of Poverty: Toward a Genealogy of Liberal Governance.* New York: Routledge.

De Bolle, M. and J. Zettelmeyer (2019) "Measuring the Rise of Economic Nationalism." Peterson Institute for International Economics, https://www.piie.com/publications/ working-papers/measuring-rise-economic-nationalism.

Delanty, G. (2006) "Nationalism and Cosmopolitanism: The Paradox of Modernity." In *The Sage Handbook of Nations and Nationalism*, edited by G. Delanty and K. Kumar, 357–69. London: Sage.

Dinnie, K. (2008) *Nation Branding: Concepts, Issues, Practice.* Oxford: Elsevier.

Dittmer, L. and S. Kim (1993) "Whither China's Quest for National Identity?" In *China's Quest for National Identity*, edited by L. Dittmer and S. Kim, 237–91. New York: Cornell University Press.

"Dolce & Gabbana Ad with Chopsticks Provokes Public Outrage in China." Goats and Soda, NPR, 1 December 2018, https://www.npr.org/sections/goatsandsoda/2018 /12/01/671891818/dolce-gabbana-ad-with-chopsticks-provokes-public-outrage-in -china.

"Dolce & Gabbana Karen Mok Backlash Shows Label Is Still Struggling to Win Back China." CNN Style, Cable News Network, 21 November 2018, https://www.cnn.com /style/article/dolce-gabbana-china-backlash-intl/index.html.

"Dolce & Gabbana Still Haunted by China Debacle, Wants to Stay Independent." *Bloomberg*, 10 October 2021, https://www.bloomberg.com/news/articles/2021-10-10 /dolce-gabbana-still-haunted-by-china-debacle-wants-to-stay-independent.

Doyle, M. (1983) "Kant, Liberal Legacies, and Foreign Affairs: Parts I & II." *Philosophy and Public Affairs* 12(3): 205–35 and 12(4): 323–53.

Dudin, Mikhail N., et al. (2016) "Financial Crisis in Greece: Challenges and Threats for the Global Economy." *International Journal of Economics and Financial Issues* 6(5): 1–6.

Durvasula, S., J. C. Andrews, and R. G. Netemeyer (1997) "A Cross-cultural Comparison of Consumer Ethnocentrism in the United States and Russia." *Journal of International Consumer Marketing* 9(4): 73–93.

Economist. "Multinational Firms Are Finding It Hard to Let Go of China," https:// www.economist.com/business/2022/11/24/multinational-firms-are-finding-it-hard -to-let-go-of-china.

Edensor, T. (2002) *National Identity, Popular Culture and Everyday Life.* Oxford and New York: Berg.

Elegant, S. (2007) "China's Me Generation." *The Times*, 26 July. http://www.time.com/ time/ magazine/article/0,9171,1647228-1,00.html. Viewed 18 December 2023.

Elliott, Z. (2019) "Balancing Act: China's Nationalist Consumer Boycotts." *The Interpreter*, https://www.lowyinstitute.org/the-interpreter/balancing-act-china-s-nationalist -consumer-boycotts.

Ellis, G. (2019) "Managing Risk in the New Era." *China Business Review*, Council on Foreign Relations, 14 March, https://www.chinabusinessreview.com/managing-risk -in-the-new-era/.

Eudaily, S. P. (2004) *The Present Politics of the Past: Indigenous Legal Activism and Resistance.* New York: Routledge.

Fang, C. (2022) *China's Economic Development: Implications for the World*, 1st edition. Routledge. https://doi.org/10.4324/9781003329305

Fershtman, C. and N. Gandal (1998) "The Effect of the Arab Boycott on Israel: The Automobile Market." *The RAND Journal of Economics* 29(1): 193–214.

Fewsmith, J. (1994) *Dilemmas of Reform in China: Political Conflict and Economic Debate.* Armonk: M. E. Sharpe.

French, P. (2007) "Asia-Pacific: Consumerism — China's iPod Revolution." *Ethical Corporation*, 8 March. http://www.ethicalcorp.com/content.asp?ContentID=4925. Viewed 20 December 2023.

Friedberg, A. L. (1993/1994) "Ripe for Rivalry: Prospects for Peace in a Multipolar Asia." *International Security* 18(3): 5–33.

Fong, V. (2004) "Filial Nationalism among Chinese Youth with Global Identities." *American Ethnologist* 3(1): 629–46.

Foster, R. J. (2002) *Materializing the Nation: Commodities, Consumption, and Media in Papua New Guinea.* Bloomington: Indiana University Press.

Foucault, M. (1983) "Afterword: The Subject and Power." In *Michel Foucault: Beyond Structuralism and Hermeneutics*, 2nd edition, edited by H. L. Dreyfuss and P. Rabinow, 208–26. Chicago: University of Chicago Press.

Foucault, M. (1988) "Politics and Reason." In *Michel Foucault: Politics, Philosophy, Culture*, edited by L. Kritzman, 57–85. London: Routledge.

Foucault, M. (1991) "Governmentality." In *The Foucault Effect: Studies in Governmentality*, edited by G. Burchell, C. Gordon, and P. Miller, 87–104. Hemel Hempstead: Harvester Wheatsheaf.

Gerth, K. (2003) *China Made: Consumer Culture and the Creation of the Nation.* Cambridge, MA: Harvard University Asia Center.

Gerth, K. (2004) *China Made: Consumer Culture and the Creation of the Nation.* Harvard East Asian Monographs.

Gerth, K. (2011) "Consumer Nationalism." In *Encyclopedia of Consumer Culture*, edited by D. Southerton, 280–82. London: Sage.

Gerth, K. (2013) *As China Goes, So Goes the World.* Farrar, Straus and Giroux.

Gerth, K. (2015) "Driven to Change: The Chinese State-Led Development of a Car Culture and Economy." In *Energy Transport in Green Transition: Perspectives on Ecomodernity*, edited by A. Middledun and N. Witoszek, 132–54. New York: Routledge.

Gerth, K. (2020) "Consumerism in Contemporary China." In *Faith, Finance, and Economy*, edited by T. Akram and S. Rashid. Cham: Palgrave Macmillan. https://doi.org/10 .1007/978-3-030-38784-6_5.

Gewirtz, P. (2023) "Words and Policies: 'De-risking' and China Policy." *Brookings*, 30 May, https://www.brookings.edu/articles/words-and-policies-de-risking-and-china -policy/. Accessed 8 December 2023.

Gilpin, R. G. (1984) "The Richness of the Tradition of Political Realism." *International Organization* 38(2): 287–304.

Globerman, S. (2017) "A New Era for Foreign Direct Investment?" *Multinational Business Review* 25(1): 5–10. https://doi.org/10.1108/MBR-12-2016-0047.

Gold, T. B. (1991) "Urban Private Business and China's Reforms." In *Reform and Reaction in Post-Mao China: The Road to Tiananmen*, edited by R. Baum, 84–103, New York: Routledge.

Goldenziel, J. (2023) "China's Anti-Espionage Law Raises Foreign Business Risk." *Forbes*. https://www.forbes.com/sites/jillgoldenziel/2023/07/03/chinas-anti-espionage-law -raises-foreign-business-risk/?sh=4ddc0c7b769e.

Good, L. K. and P. Huddleston (1995) "Ethnocentrism of Polish and Russian Consumers: Are Feelings and Intentions Related?" *International Marketing Review* 12(5): 35–48.

Granzin, K. L. and J. J. Painter (2001) "Motivational Influences on 'Buy Domestic' Purchasing: Marketing Management Implications from a Study of Two Nations." *Journal of International Marketing* 9(2): 73–96.

Greenfeld, L. (2006) "Modernity and Nationalism." In *The Sage Handbook of Nations and Nationalism*, edited by G. Delanty and K. Kumar, 13–34. London: Sage.

Greenfeld, L. (2012) "Nationalism and Terrorism." Project Syndicate Online. project -syndicate.org.

Gregory, T. E. (1931) "Economic Nationalism. Address given at Chatham House, March 12." *International Affairs (Royal Institute for International Affairs 1931–39)* 10(3): 289–306.

Gries, P. H. (2004) *Chinese New Nationalism: Pride, Politics, and Diplomacy*. Berkeley: University of California Press.

Gries, P. H. (2005) "Nationalism and Chinese Foreign Policy." In *China Rising: Power and Motivation in Chinese Foreign Policy*, edited by Y. Deng and F. L. Wang, 103–20. Lanham, MD: Rowman & Littlefield.

Hamin, H. and G. Elliott (2006) "A Less-Developed Country Perspective of Consumer Ethnocentrism and 'Country of Origin Effects': Indonesian Evidence." *Asia Pacific Journal of Marketing and Logistics* 18: 9–92.

Hang, N. T. T. (2017) "The Rise of China: Challenges, Implications, and Options for the United States." *Indian Journal of Asian Affairs* 30(1/2): 47–64, http://www.jstor.org /stable/26465816.

He, B. (2003) "China's National Identity: A Source of Conflict between Democracy and State Nationalism." In *Nationalism, Democracy and National Integration in China*, edited by L. H. Liew and S. Wang, 170–92. London: Routledge.

Heilperin, M. A. (1960) *Studies in Economic Nationalism*. Geneva: L'Institut Universitaire de Hautes Études Internatio- nales.

Helleiner, E. (2002) "Economic Nationalism as a Challenge to Economic Liberalism? Lessons from the 19th Century." *International Studies Quarterly* 46: 307–29.

Helleiner, E. (2005) "Why would Nationalists not want a National Currency? The Case of Quebec." In *Economic Nationalism in a Globalizing World*, edited by E. Helleiner and A. Pickel, 164–18. Ithaca: Cornell University Press.

Hernandez, J. C. (2019) "Fashion Labels Apologize for Implying Taiwan and Hong Kong Independent from China." *The Guardian*, 12 August, https://www.theguardian.com /world/2019/aug/12/fashion-labels-apologise-for-implying-taiwan-and-hong-kong -independent-from-china.

Hieronymi, O. (1980) *The New Economic Nationalism*. Geneva: Battelle Geneva Research Center.

Hobsbawm, E. (1983) "Introduction: The Invention of Tradition." In *The Invention of Tradition*, edited by E. Hobsbawm and T. Ranger, 1–14. Cambridge: Cambridge University Press.

Holzer, B. (2006) "Political Consumerism between Individual Choice and Collective Action: Social Movements, Role Mobilization and Signalling." *International Journal of Consumer Studies* 30(5): 405–15.

胡锡进. "我们不应让MINI的事情过度发酵." Wenxuecity, 22 April 2023, https://m.wenxuecity.com/news/2023/04/22/12276407.html.

Huddleston, P., L. K. Good, and L. Stoel (2001) "Consumer Ethnocentrism, Product Necessity and Polish Consumers' Perceptions of Quality." *International Journal of Retail & Distribution Management* 29(5): 236–46.

Hunwick, R. F. (2014) "Why Christmas Is Huge in China." *The Atlantic*, 24 December.

Javalgi, R. G., V. P. Khare, A. Gross, and R. F. Schere (2005) "An Application of the Consumer Ethnocentrism Model to French Consumers." *International Business Review* 14(3): 325–44.

Jiang, M. Y. (2021) "Implications of the New Wave of Nationalism in the People's Republic of China for Australian Companies." Australia-China Relations Institute, https://www.australiachinarelations.org/sites/default/files/202106%20Perspectives_Implications%20of%20the%20new%20wave%20of%20nationalism%20on%20the%20People%27s%20Republic%20of%20China%20for%20Australian%20companies_Dr%20Maggie%20Ying%20Jiang.pdf.

Jiang, Y. (2012) *Cybernationalism in China: Challenging Western Media Portrayal of Censorship*. Adelaide: University of Adelaide Press.

Jiang, Y. (2014) "Reversed Agenda-setting Effects in China Case Studies of Weibo Trending Topics and the Effects on State-owned Media in China." *The Journal of International Communication* 20(2): 168–83, https://doi.org/10.1080/13216597.2014.908785.

Jiménez-Guerrero, J. F., et al. (2020) "Alternative Proposals to Measure Consumer Ethnocentric Behavior: A Narrative Literature Review." *Sustainability* 12(6): 2216.

Johnson, A. (1917) "The Passing of Economic Nationalism." *Harper's Magazine* 135(806): 221–25.

Johnson, H. G., ed. (1967) *Economic Nationalism in Old and New States*. London: Allen & Unwin.

Ju, H. (2007) "The Nature of Nationalism in the 'Korean Wave: A Framing Analysis of News Coverage about Korean Pop Culture'," http://www.allacademic.com/meta/p187925_index.html. Accessed 15 June 2009.

Kahan, A. (1967) "Nineteenth-Century European Experience with Policies of Economic Nationalism." In *Economic Nationalism in Old and New States*, 1st edition, edited by Taylors Johnson, 17–31. H.G. Routledge. https://doi.org/10.4324/9781003195665.

Kania-Lundholm, M. (2014) "Nation in Market Times: Connecting the National and the Commercial. A Research Overview." *Sociology Compass* 8(6): 603–13.

Koetse, M. (2023) "BMW Ice Cream Gate: Three Reasons Why a MINI Story Became a Major Incident, What's on Weibo." https://www.whatsonweibo.com/bmw-ice-cream-gate-three-reasons-why-a-mini-story-became-a-major-incident/. Accessed 30 November 2023.

Kristof, N. D. (1993) "The Rise of China." *Foreign Affairs* 72(5): 59–73.

Lantz, G. and S. Loeb (1996) "Country of Origin and Ethnocentrism: An Analysis of Canadian and American Preferences using Social Identity Theory." *Advances in Consumer Research* 23: 374–8.

Lasch, C. (2018) *Culture of Narcissism: American Life in an Age of Diminishing Expectations*. Warner Books.

Lee, K. (2023) "G-7 Leaders de-risk China." CNBC, 22 May, https://www.cnbc.com /2023.

Li, C. (1998) *China: The Consumer Revolution.* New York: John Wiley and Sons.

Li, H. (2009) "Marketing Japanese Products in the Context of Chinese Nationalism." *Critical Studies in Media Communication* 26(5): 435–56.

Li, J. (2018) "China's Young Consumers are Snubbing Foreign Brands Amid Growing National Pride, Says Credit Suisse." *South China Morning Post.* https://www.scmp.com /business/china-business/article/2138267/chinas-young-consumers-are-snubbing -foreign-brands-amid. Viewed 22 March 2023.

Li, J. (2019) "The Impact of Economic Nationalism on Foreign Investment in China." *International Business Review* 28(5): 819–27.

Liu, P. (2021) "Chinese Patriotism Is New Sales Octane as Millennials Embrace Home-Grown Brands at the Expense of Foreign Icons." *South China Morning Post.* https:// www.scmp.com/business/china-business/article/3048428/chinese-patriotism-new -sales-octane-millennials-embrace. Viewed 01 February 2023.

Livingston, S. (2020) "The Chinese Communist Party Targets the Private Sector". https://www.csis.org/analysis/chinese-communist-party-targets-private-sector.

Lu, Y. (2018) "The Triggers of Nationalism in China: A Critical Review." *China Review* 18(2): 77–100.

Macesich, G. (1985) *Economic Nationalism and Stability.* New York: Praeger.

Marín, S. C. (2005) *El Origen Doméstico de los productos como ventaja competitiva: La Etnocentricidad del consumidor.* Spain: Universitat de València Servei de Publicacions.

McEwen, S. (1994) "New Kids on the Block." *China Business Review* 21(3): 35–9.

McKinsey. (2023). "The New Challenges for MNCs in China." https://www.mckinsey .com/mgi/our-research/the-china-imperative-for-multinational-companies.

McKinsey Global Institute. "The China Imperative for Multinational Companies," https://www.mckinsey.com/mgi/our-research/the-china-imperative-for -multinational-companies. Accessed 11 August 2023.

Min, Q. (1989) *Zhongguo zhengzhi wenhua* [Political Culture in China]. Kunming: Yunnan renmin chubanshe.

Morrissey, R. (2012) "China's Ye Shiwen Raises Doping Suspicion with 'Impossible' Win." *Chicago Sun-Times,* 31 July, http://www.suntimes.com/sports/olympics/14121090-777/ story.html. Accessed 12 August 2023.

Nakano, T. (2004) "Theorising Economic Nationalism." *Nation and Nationalism* 10(3): 211–29.

Naughton, B. (1995) *Growing Out of the Plan: Chinese Economic Reform, 1978–1993.* Cambridge University Press.

"NBA Will Lose Hundreds of Millions of Dollars Due to Rift with China, Commissioner Says." CNBC, 11 October 2019, https://www.cnbc.com/2019/10/11/nba-will-lose -hundreds-of-millions-of-dollars-due-to-rift-with-china-commissioner-says.html.

"NBA-China Feud: Timeline of Actions over Daryl Morey Tweet." Business Insider, 22 October 2019, https://www.businessinsider.com/nba-china-feud-timeline-hong-kong -protests-daryl-morey-tweet-2019-10.

Neilson, L. A. (2010) "Boycott or Buycott? Understanding Political Consumerism." *Journal of Consumer Behaviour* 9(3): 214–27.

NetEase News. (2008) "Shanghai nan zi shao qian xian fu [Shanghai Man Burning Money to Show Off His Richness]." 23 October. http://news.163.com/06/1023/17 /2U4R9BGQ00011229. html. Viewed 20 December 2023.

Nielsen, J. A. and M. T. Spence (1997) "A Test of the Stability of the Cetscale, a Measure of Consumers' Ethnocentric Tendencies." *Journal of Marketing Theory and Practice* 5(4): 68–76. http://www.jstor.org/stable/40469851

OECD (2022) *OECD Economic Outlook, Interim Report March 2022: Economic and Social Impacts and Policy Implications of the War in Ukraine.* Paris: Organisation for Economic Co-operation and Development, https://www.oecd-ilibrary.org/sites/4181d61ben/index.html?itemId=/content/publication/4181d61b-en. Accessed 10 March 2023.

Okechuku, C. (1994) "The Importance of Product Country of Origin: A Conjoint Analysis of the United States, Canada, Germany and The Netherlands." *European Journal of Marketing* 28(4): 5–19.

Olins, W. (1999) *Trading Identities: Why Countries and Companies are Taking on Each Others' Roles.* London: Foreign Policy Centre.

Orazi, F. (2022) "The Elusiveness of Nationalism." *Revue Française de Civilisation Britannique* [Online] XXVII-2, Online since 15 June 2022, connection on 04 February 2023, http://journals.openedition.org/rfcb/9353. https://doi.org/10.4000/rfcb.9353.

Owen, J. M. (1994) "How Liberalism Produces Democratic Peace." *International Security* 19(2): 87–125.

Ozili, P. K. (2022) "Global Economic Consequence of Russian Invasion of Ukraine." SSRN, https://ssrn.com/abstract=4064770.

Paek, H-J. and Pan, Z. (2004) "Spreading Global Consumerism: Effects of Mass Media and Advertising on Consumerist Values in China." *Mass Communication and Society* 7(4): 491–515. https://doi.org/10.1207/s15327825mcs0704_7.

Pak, J. H. (2020) "China's Approach to South Korea, Global China: Assessing China's Global Role in the World." https://www.brookings.edu/wp-content/uploads/2020/07/FP_20200606_china_south_korea_pak_v2.pdf.

Pickel, A. (2003) "Explaining, and Explaining with, Economic Nationalism." *Nations and Nationalism* 9(1): 105–27.

Pickel, A. and J. True (2002) "Global, Transnational and National Change Mechanisms: Bridging International and Comparative Approaches to Post-communist Transformation." In *Postcommunist Transformation and the Social Sciences: Cross-disciplinary Approaches*, edited by F. Bonker, K. Muller, and A. Pickel, 153–73. Boulder: Rowman & Littlefield.

Pye, L. (1996) "How China's Nationalism was Shanghaied." In *Chinese Nationalism*, edited by J. Unger, 86–112. Armonk, New York: M. E. Sharpe.

Qiu, Z. Q. (2010) "Technology Progress and Social Change." In *Thirty Years of Reform and Social Changes in China*, edited by Qiang Li, 335–71. Brill.

QQ News. (2008) "Ni maiguo ma: Xiaobailing hua xueben mai shenchipin de xinli mimi [Did You Ever Buy It: The White Collars' Psychological Secret of Buying Luxuries]." 15 May. http://finance.qq.com/a/20080515/001429.htm. Viewed 20 December 2023.

Quirk, J. (2022) "Has Neoliberal Globalisation Contributed to Growing Levels of Nationalism Across Europe?" *Australian and New Zealand Journal of European Studies* 14(1). https://doi.org/10.30722/anzjes.vol14.iss1.15857.

Rammal, H. G., E. L. Rose, P. N. Ghauri, P. D. Ørberg Jensen, M. Kipping, B. Petersen, and M. Scerri (2022) "Economic Nationalism and Internationalization of Services: Review and Research Agenda." *Journal of World Business* 57(3). ISSN 1090-9516. https://doi.org/10.1016/j.jwb.2022.101314.

Ramzy, A. (2012) "Doping Suspicions about Gold-medal Swimmer Trigger Angry Response in China." *Time*, 3 July, http://olympics.time.com/2012/07/31/doping-suspicions-about-gold-medal-swimer-trigger-angryresponse-in-china/#ixzz2PNVTM1Lq. Accessed 11 August 2013.

Rappard, W. E. (1937) "Economic Nationalism." In *Authority and the Individual*, 74–112. Cambridge: Harvard Tercentenary Publications.

Reich, R. B. (1991) *The Work of Nations. Preparing Ourselves for 21st-Century Capitalism.* New York. Simon & Schuster Ltd.

Rein, S. (2017) *The War for China's Wallet: Profiting from the New World Order.* De Gruyter.

Riskin, C. (1987) *China's Political Economy: The Quest for Development Since 1949.* Oxford: Oxford University Press.

Rose, N. (1999b) "Preface to the Second Edition." In *Governing the Soul: The Shaping of the Private Self*, 2nd edition, edited by N. Rose, xxi–xxii. London: Free Associations Books.

Roy, D. (1995) "Assessing the Asian-Pacific 'Power Vacuum'." *Survival* 37(3): 45–60.

Russell, F. (2021) "China Consumers Continue to Boost E-Commerce Spending: Bain & Kantar." *Forbes.* https://www.forbes.com/sites/russellflannery/2021/06/29/china-consumers-continue-to-boost-e-commerce-spending-bain--kantar/?sh=54f9ed9a2c85. Viewed 21 January 2024.

Russett, B. (1993) *Grasping the Democratic Peace: Principles for a Post-Cold War World.* Princeton, NJ: Princeton University Press.

Samoui, F. (2009) "Effet de l'origine perçue du nom de marque sur les perceptions du consommateur: cas du consommateur de pays émergents." *8th International Congress Marketing Trends, Paris*, 27.

Segal, G. (1995) "Rising Nationalism in China Worries the Japanese." *International Herald Tribune* 28 (September): 10.

Seo, J. (2007) "Internal Dynamics of Chinese Nationalism and Northeast Asian Regional Order." In *Korean Security in a Changing East Asia*, edited by T. Roehrig, J. Seo, and U. Heo, 114–35. Praeger: Security International.

Seo, J. (2008) "Manufacturing Nationalism in China: Political Economy of 'Say No' Businesses," http://www.allacademic.com/meta/p251595_index.html. Accessed 15 June 2010.

Shankarmahesh, M. N. (2006) "Consumer Ethnocentrism: An Integrative Review of its Antecedents and Consequences." *Journal of International Marketing Review* 23(2): 146–72.

Sharma, P. (2015) "Consumer Ethnocentrism: Reconceptualization and Cross-Cultural Validation." *Journal of International Business Studies* 46(3): 381–9.

Sharma, S., T. Shimp, and J. Shin (1995) "Consumer Ethnocentrism, a Test of Antecedents and Moderators." *Journal of the Academy of Marketing Science* 23(1): 26–37.

Shimp, T. A. (1984) "Consumer Ethnocentrism: The Concept and a Preliminary Empirical Test." *Association for Consumer Research* 11: 285–90.

Shimp, T. A. and S. Sharma (1987) "Consumer Ethnocentrism: Construction and Validation of the CETSCALE." *Journal of Marketing Research* 24(3): 280–89.

Siamagka, N.-T. and G. Balabanis (2015) "Revisiting Consumer Ethnocentrism: Review, Reconceptualization, and Empirical Testing." *Journal of International Marketing* 23(3): 66–86.

Silili, E. P. and A. C. Karunaratna (2014) "Consumer Ethnocentrism: Tendency of Sri Lankan Youngsters." *Global Journal of Emerging Trends in e-Business, Marketing and Consumer Psychology* 1(1): 1–15.

Singh, P. (2022) "How Exclusionary Nationalism Has Made the World Socially Sicker from COVID-19." *Nationalities Papers* 50(1): 104–17, https://doi.org/10.1017/nps.2021 .36.

Stevenson, T. (2018) "How Dolce & Gabbana Lost 98% of Their Chinese Market with One Video." *Better Marketing*, 19 November, https://qz.com/quartzy/1474631/dolce -gabbanas-racism-debacle-in-china-could-cost-it-a-fortune/.

Strizhakova, Y., R. A. Coulter, and L. Price (2008) "Branded Products as a Passport to Global Citizenship: Perspectives from Developed and Developing Countries." *Journal of International Marketing* 16(4): 57–85.

Suh, T. and I. G. Kwon (2002) "Globalization and Reluctant Buyers." *International Marketing Review* 19(6): 663–80.

Sun, L. P. (1996) "Huiru shijie zhuliu wenming-minzu zhuyi santi [Flowing Together with the World's Mainstream Civilization]." *DF* 1, 15–19.

Talbot, S. (1996) "Democracy and the National Interest." *Foreign Affairs* 75(6): 47–63.

Teiwes, F. and W. Sun (2015) *Paradoxes of Post-Mao Rural Reform: Initial Steps toward a New Chinese Countryside, 1976–1981.* Routledge.

Tian, K. and L. Dong (2011) *Consumer-Citizens of China: The Role of Foreign Brands in the Imagined Future China.* Routledge.

"Top Challenges for Doing Business in China." TMF Group, 9 May 2022, https://www .tmf-group.com/en/news-insights/business-culture/top-challenges-china/.

Turner, G. (2010) "The Banality of Commercial Nationalism." Presentation to the Annual Convention of the International Communication Association, Singapore, June 21–25, 2010.

Vida, A. F. (1999) "Factors Underlying the Phenomenon of Consumer Ethnocentricity: Evidence from Four Central European Countries." *The International Review of Retail, Distribution and Consumer Research* 9(4): 321–37.

Volcic, Z. (2009) "Television in the Balkans: The Rise of Commercial Nationalism." In *Television Studies after TV: Understanding Television in the Post-Broadcast Era*, edited by G. Turner and J. Tay, 115–24. London: Routledge.

Volcic, Z. and M. Andrejevic (2011) "Nation Branding in the Era of Commercial Nationalism." *International Journal of Communication* 5: 598–618.

Volčič, Z. and M. Andrejevic (2015) *Commercial Nationalism: Selling the Nation and Nationalizing the Sell.* Basingstoke: Palgrave Macmillan.

Wang, S. G. (2003) "Nationalism and Democracy: Second Thoughts." 30 May. www .cuhk.edu.hk/gpa/wang_files/Nationalism&Dem.doc, viewed 7 March 2009.

Wang, J. (2006) "Consumer Nationalism and Corporate Reputation Management in the Global Era." *Corporate Communications* 10(3): 223–39.

Wang, Z. (2021) "Nationalism and Cultural Insensitivity in Cross-cultural Marketing: Evidence from China." *Asia Pacific Journal of Management* 38(2): 261–74.

Wang, C. L. and Z. X. Chen (2004) "Consumer Ethnocentrism and Willingness to Buy Domestic Products in a Developing Country Setting: Testing Moderating Effects." *Journal of Consumer Marketing* 21(6): 391–400.

Wei, C. X. G., X. Y. Liu, and W. C. Kirby (2002) *Exploring Nationalisms of China: Themes and Conflicts.* Lanham, MD: Greenwood Publishing Group.

Wetzels, M., K. De Ruyter, and M. Van Birgelen (1998) "Marketing Service Relationships: The Role of Commitment." *Journal of Business & Industrial Marketing* 13(4/5): 406–23.

White, L. (2009) "The Man from Snowy River: Australia's Bush Legend and Commercial Nationalism." *Tourism Review International* 13(2): 139–46.

Woods, E. T., R. Schertzer, L. Greenfeld, C. Hughes, and C. Miller-Idriss (2020) "COVID-19, Nationalism, and the Politics of Crisis: A Scholarly Exchange." *Nations and Nationalism* 26: 807–25. https://doi.org/10.1111/nana.12644.

Woody, C. (2017) "China is Going after South Korea's Wallet in their Dispute over the THAAD Missile System." Business Insider, https://www.businessinsider.com/china-south-korea-economic-boycott-protests-over-thaad-missile-system-2017-3.

Xinhua (2021) "Pic Story: Change in Chinese Consumption Behavior over Past Decades," China.org.cn. Accessed 30 June 2022.

Xu, Y. J., et al. (2018) *Chinese Consumers and the Fashion Market*. Springer Series in Fashion Business.

Yang, F. (2016) "Rethinking Commercial Nationalism: The 'Chinese Dream' in Neoliberal Globalization." In *Commercial Nationalism. Palgrave Studies in Communication for Social Change*, edited by Z. Volcic and M. Andrejevic. London: Palgrave Macmillan. https://doi.org/10.1057/9781137500991_5.

Yang, Y. (2021) "Social Media Influencers Help Chinese Brands Outfox Foreign Rivals." *Financial Times.* https://www.ft.com/content/25ab5f9f-0cf9-4c2b-aed6-990aff95c34c. Viewed 26 June 2023.

Young, S. (1995) *Private Business and Economic Reform in China*, 6. Routledge.

Yuanhang, R. (1957a) "Shucai diqi bufen nongmin zizhang langfei xianxiang" (The Phenomenon of Vegetable Farmers Overspending). *Hangzhou Daily*, 25 July.

Yuanhang, R. (1957b) "Qian yao yong zai daokou shang" (Money Ought to Be Spent on the Blade). *Hangzhou Daily*, 22 August.

Yu, S. and W. Kane. (2021) "Analysis: Chinese Flock to Home-Grown Brands in Golden Opportunity for Investors." *Reuters.* https://www.reuters.com/business/finance/chinese-flock-home-grown-brands-golden-opportunity-investors-2021-06-27/. Viewed 27 June 2023.

Zaagman, E. (2019) "China's Own "Great Delusion." *The Interpreter,* https://www.lowyinstitute.org/the-interpreter/china-s-own-great-delusion.

Zhang, X. D. (2001) *Whither China? Intellectual Politics in Contemporary China*. Durham, NC: Duke University Press.

Zhao, D. X. (2002) "An Angle on Nationalism in China Today: Attitudes among Students after Belgrade 1999." *China Quarterly* 172: 885–905.

Zhao, S. S. (2005) "Nationalism's Double Edge." *The Wilson Quarterly,* Autumn. http://74.125.155.132/search?q=cache:R5fCpvYI6BAJ:www.wilsoncenter.org/index.   cfm%3Ffuseaction%3Dwq.print%26essay_id%3D146859%26stoplayout%3Dtrue+   nationalism+is+a+double-edged+sword&cd=7&hl=zh-CN&ct=clnk. Viewed 29 December 2023.

Zheng, Y. N. (1999) *Discovering Chinese Nationalism in China: Modernization, Identity, and International Relations*. Cambridge: Cambridge University Press.

Zhou, K. X. (1996) *How the Farmers Changed China: Power of the People*. Westview Press.

Zhou, Y. M. (2005b) "Informed Nationalism: Military Websites in Chinese Cyberspace." *Journal of Contemporary China* 14: 543–62.

INDEX

Note: Numbers in bold font refers to figures & tables

Milton Keynes UK
Ingram Content Group UK Ltd.
UKHW040645290824
447361UK00002B/7